LOVE STORIES OF WAR HEROES

The book is a collection of fifteen love stories of war heroes. Each story depicts the greatest example of patriotism and bravery with its characters drawing strength from their women. This book is an experiment to prove that the biggest source of energy that makes daring war heroes is actually love. It is a testimony of the existence of the most sensitive minds inside tough bodies. Certain delicate issues are addressed and natural solutions offered. The stories are replete with profound emotions and the smooth flow of events that touch the hearts of the readers.

LOVE STORIES OF WAR HEROES

Col Gopal Purdhani (Retd)

A Sterling Paperbacks

STERLING PAPERBACKS
An imprint of
Sterling Publishers (P) Ltd.
A-59, Okhla Industrial Area, Phase-II,
New Delhi-110020.
Tel: 26387070, 26386209; Fax: 91-11-26383788
E-mail: sterlingpublishers@touchtelindia.net
ghai@nde.vsnl.net.in
www.sterlingpublishers.com

Love Stories of War Heroes
Copyright © 2006 by Col Gopal Purdhani
ISBN 81 207 3051 8

All rights are reserved. No part of this publication
may be reproduced, stored in a retrieval system
or transmitted, in any form or by any means,
mechanical, photocopying, recording or otherwise,
without prior written permission
of the original publisher.

Published by Sterling Publishers Pvt. Ltd., New Delhi-110 020.
Printed at Sterling Publishers Pvt. Ltd., New Delhi-110020.

Preface

Some of the daring war heroes have been dwelling in my mind permanently, though they remained unsung for a very long time. Those Indian soldiers were the true sons of the soil who willingly sacrificed their lives for the sake of our country and welcomed their end as much as they rejoiced the life which they lived fully and for every single moment.

Their sweet memories always kept pricking my heart with sorrow until now, when I found the release. They would always be excellent examples of patriotism, sacrifice, valour and inspiration to all the soldiers. I am sure that every reader would empathise with and relate to each one of them in her or his own sentiments and experiences and share them with me.

In writing this book I also aim to highlight various aspects of army life, particularly its sensitive and delicate sides, so as to encourage the young minds to accept the challenges that may come their way at some time or other in the future. The romantic exploits of brave heroes showed how humane they were.

I have also tried to exemplify the greatest instance of national integration that exists in the Indian army.

Further, the stories show that the love and affection which the troops received from their near and dear ones, and from their countrymen, was their main wellspring of moral resolve, and thus brought them victory in the battlefield.

My imagination gave them birth. Their stories are absolutely fresh and poignantly relevant to modern warfare.

This is my humble tribute to the gallant "Unknown Soldier."

Col. Gopal Purdhani (Retd)
Magistrate, Delhi

Acknowledgements

If I could quantify, ninety nine percent of my gratitude would be for those beautiful women who showered their love on my war heroes, inspiring them to fight for the nation, fearlessly and with total dedication. My remaining gratitude would go to my family members and friends who became my real inspiration and who have kept reminding me to tell their stories to the world.

I am indebted to Lt. Gen. T. J. S. Gill, PVSM, Lt. Gen. B. K. Bopanna, PVSM, AVSM, VSM, and Maj. Gen. K. C. Mehra, AVSM, and Surgeon Rear Admiral P. Sivdas, AVSM, who wrote the foreword of the book and expressed that it would touch the hearts of the readers.

I convey my sincere thanks to Padma Bhushan Lt. Gen. B. N. Shahi, PVSM, AVSM, VSM (then DGAFMS), Lt. Gen. J. R. Bhardwaj, PVSM, AVSM, VSM, PHS (Ex-DGAFMS), Lt. Gen. R. S. Shahrawat, AVSM, VSM (Ex-DGOS), Maj. Gen. S. K. Sanan, AVSM, VSM, (Ex-Judge Advocate General), Maj. Gen. Nilendra Kumar, VSM (Present Judge Advocate General), Maj. Gen. S. K. Sen, VSM, Addl. Director General APS, and Brig. Y. S. Mohan, VSM, DDG APS, for sparing their valuable time for discussions on their respective subjects and for rendering the most valuable technical advice. I convey deep gratitude to Mr. Ingo Porada of South Africa for editing the book.

My Dear Nation

Nation; Oh my dear Nation,
    You are the pure innocence of a child,
        and the shining smile of a beautiful damsel,
            I offer to you pouring love from my heart,
                and highly excited longing desire of Service.

Nation; Oh my dar Nation,
    You are the prestigious veil of my wife,
        and the radiant face of my dear daughter,
            You are the beautiful smile of my son,
                and the best friend like his honest love.

Nation; Oh my dear Nation,
    You are the piece of land of my sky,
        and the transparent curtain of the sun,
            You are the enchanting face of the moon,
                and the bed of the sprawling moon light.

Nation; Oh my dear Nation,
    All that I have really belongs to you,
        and I owe to you each drop of my blood,
            With feeling of exuberance and enthusiasm,
            I am now ready to pay my debts to you.

Contents

1. The 1965 War — 1
2. My War Hero — 10
3. Love without Response has No Life — 17
4. Love of Three Generations — 26
5. Love Affairs of Some Enemy Soldiers — 31
6. One Life is Not Enough for Love — 37
7. Double Standards — 80
8. Delayed Letter — 84
9. The Enemy within the Country — 95
10. Love Triangle — 107
11. Sainik Veer Singh — 114
12. Human Sacrifice — 119
13. Let Love Be the Winner — 125
14. The Story Tellers — 135
15. Never Say Die — 142

1

The 1965 War

My story of how I took part in the war with Pakistan in 1965 seems to me like a story of yesterday. I was twenty two years old then, a second lieutenant with one star on each of my shoulders; and I felt on top of world with exuberance and pride. I was the youngest and latest to join my unit. The other officers used to call me "Palton Munnu" - unit kid.

Before the war started, my unit was located on the outskirts of a big city in Madhya Pradesh. Our daily drill always started with physical training in the early morning, education classes in the forenoon, small arms firing practice in the afternoon, and sand model discussions or meetings in the evening. Twice a month we used to have late night route marches to improve our endurance for the night campaigns.

At 10:00 p.m. on one evening in late August 1965, it was 10:00 p.m. when the commanding officer (CO) was summoned for an urgent meeting by the General Officer Commanding (GOC). The 'Old Man' instructed us to keep hanging around in the officers' mess until he returned; he said that he may come back with some good news.

We re-filled our glasses and eagerly anticipated the good news. A hot discussion followed on music and movies. Women and politics are not discussed in the army officers' messes.

The Old Man returned at about 2:00 a.m. We noticed an unusual twist to his moustache, and a smile, both on his lips and in his eyes. His chest had swelled up. He signalled to us to make a half circle around him.

"Gentlemen," he roared, standing upright, with both hands on his hips, "the moment for which every soldier keeps himself prepared has arrived. I applaud all of you on the orders to move to the battlefield for the war ... ."

"Hey ha, hey ha, hey ha ... *Bharat mata ki jai* ... ." We started singing and dancing. The calm atmosphere of the sleepy night was suddenly punctuated by our joyous noise. The cook Abdul Rahim, *masalchi* (the dish washer) Sewa Singh, and other waiters gathered around us. We hugged each other. The lights started shining in the neighbouring buildings.

"Well done, well done. I am happy, I am very happy to see your *josh*. We can beat any enemy on this earth. Well done, boys. Keep it up. The whole nation is looking at us for the real test. We will win it to prove it. And there is something else. We are moving for the attack to our Palton Munnu's native place Jammu."

"Hey ha, hey ha ... ." I found myself jumping to the middle of the circle and dancing. "Hey ha, hey ha ... ." Everybody joined me. We noticed tears of joy in the eyes of the Old Man. He too joined us in dancing to "Hey ha ... hey ha."

Rounds of liquor followed till 3:00 a.m., when dinner was finally served. The CO briefed us on the move at the dining table.

The next day was very busy. We had already prepared the load tables. All our luggage, boxes, equipment and other articles were prominently marked with vehicle numbers. All the personnel also knew in which vehicle or railway compartment they were to travel. Every vehicle was earmarked and allotted to a particular driver. The load table plan was put into effect. So, there was no confusion; there were no problems.

One contingent with light equipment known as 'advance party' was lifted by air. More than four-fifths of the troops and equipment were to leave by the army special train. The railway authorities were very prompt in placing passenger bogies and goods wagons at our disposal.

I was to travel by train and was appointed train-adjutant (administrative officer in charge of the train). Our second-in-command was designated as commanding officer of the train.

On the way, wherever our train stopped for refilling water or for other needs, the local people rushed to meet us in large numbers. They greeted us, cheered us and said encouraging words to boost our morale. The elders shook their hands and hugged us, and the old ladies applied *tilak* (red colour) on our foreheads and blessed us. Young girls tied *rakhis* (sacred-coloured threads) on our wrists, and those who could not find threads tore off a piece of cloth from their *chunri* (scarf) to make a *rakhi*.

The people brought us sweets, fruits, milk, tea, biscuits, food, pickle, and many other things. In the hurry, they gave us whatever they could lay their hands on. Even the small children brought their toys as gifts for us. I remember that a six years or seven years-old child gave me his broken wooden gun.

For some time, the people would stand on the railway tracks to stop our train and serve us tea, coffee or milk; then they hurriedly cleared our way so that we could proceed further.

The tide of love was flowing in abundance. Irrespective of cast or creed, the people showered their love on us like a father or mother or brother or sister. We realised that the entire population of our country was one large family to whom we belonged and whom we had to protect. That was enough for me and all other soldiers to spurn us on 'do or die' for the country.

In those days the rail-head was Pathankot; hence we changed over to marching contingents from there. My village was on the way of our route. The word had gone around that I was in a military contingent on a particular day. People from my village and all nearby villages gathered on the road. They encircled me and my colleagues. They hugged us, tapped our back, gave us sweets and showered their love on us.

My father spoke loudly: "Son, remember, if the nation needs you, then we do not need you." There was clapping by all. There was big noise and my relatives and young friends were in a great mood.

My eyes were searching for my fiancée Dharti in the crowd. I noticed that she was standing in a corner. A simple and 'chhui mui' (shy) type village belle, she was looking at me with wide open blank eyes. We had immense love for each other. Our parents had decided to celebrate our marriage on the next Baisakhi day (13 April).

I rushed to her and shook her shoulders: "Hey, *Dharti ma*, you also say something."

"What can I say?" she asked.

"Say some thing, *yaar*, anything. I am going to fight a war. Aren't you excited, dumb girl?" I asked.

"Yes, I am also excited. I cannot make out what to say on such occasions," she managed to utter.

"Say something, and please hurry up. Be quick, we cannot stop here for long. You can at least wish me good luck for destroying the enemy and capturing a lot of land," I said.

She said, "Dharti, you have already won. And now, wherever your steps will fall, that land will be yours. You will be victorious. God be with you always," she wished; and continued, "please listen; I have a letter for you. Read it, whenever you get time." And she quietly handed over an almost mutilated piece of paper to me. From the condition of the paper I could guess what was going on in her mind. I kept her letter in my pocket.

She touched my feet like a devoted wife. I also bowed down and touched her feet. Everybody started laughing.

"Naughty." My father laughed and started wiping his eyes.

"*Eh, Dharti mata*, look after the old man," I told her.

"Which old man? May be my *sambandhi* (father of my fiancée), is an old man, not me ... I am still young." My father tried to raise a laugh as he twisted his moustache. All started laughing. With such emotions, I found myself fully charged to plunge into any adventure.

With loud slogans like "*Bharat mata ki jai, Dharti mata ki jai,*" we marched on. During the advance I forgot about the letter. We had become almost like robots, totally mechanical humans, and the thought of tiredness or fatigue never crossed our minds. I do not exactly remember when I read that letter for the first time; but after the ceasefire, I read the letter many a times, every day.

She had written, "my love, on the day of our engagement I had accepted you as my husband in my mind and soul. That is why I have told you to apply *sindoor* (red colour) on my forehead when we visited the temple later in the evening. My marriage with you has already taken place. Only the formality by the *punditji* remains. I will live as your wife, and - God forbid - if you do not come back from the war, I will die as a widow of a brave soldier like you. Remember that you should be the winner. Kill the enemy. Be Arjun, not only Abhimanyu, because I want you to be brave and win. Do not let the enemy cross our borders, because if that happens, your Dharti, along with others, will also become the captive of the enemy.

"I know that you will come back. You must come back to me, and then the new day will commence. Until then it is night for me, a lonely dark night. Stay awake throughout the night for as long the war is on. Keep in mind that someone is waiting for you. That will always make you feel 'not to say die.' May God be with you always, until your victory.

"With all my love,
"Yours only,
"Dharti."

On 3 September 1965, Pakistan attacked India. The war had been declared. We were deployed near Jammu to cross the Pakistan border on the Pathankot-Jammu National Highway. This area was known as 'Sialkot Sector.'

The terrain was fully flat and intensely cultivated on both sides of the border. Sugarcane and maize crops had fully grown up. There were no hills, no forests. The war was to be fought in the fields in that sector.

The first village of Pakistan which we captured on D-Day (the first day of attack) was known as Dharwa. We found that all the villagers were hiding inside the primary school building. We allowed the civilians to flee to safer places.

The next village also fell to us in a similar way. We asked them why they had not run away. We were told that their army authorities had announced that they had already captured Jammu and Pathankot. Thus they had risked the lives of their civilians with false propaganda.

Most of our advances were made during the night. During the day time enemy air attacks were very frequent, but that did not deter us from advancing. The moves of marching contingents are generally covered by artillery gunfire or by tanks, or sometimes by advance air strikes.

It was heartening to see huge Indian Sherman tanks smashing away the Pakistani Patton tanks. Like the Khem-Karan Sector in Punjab, the Sialkot Sector also became thunder-battlefield all over. Our armour regiments played havoc with enemy tanks. But importance of the infantry can never be overlooked, because it is actually the infantry which captures and physically holds the ground.

We had witnessed some very thrilling incidences during war. On one such occasion, our boys mounted an enemy tank and captured it in perfect running condition, after killing all the occupants with small arms. The medium machine gun was dismounted from the tank along with bullet belts. The machine gun was handed over to our company, and we amused ourselves by firing Pakistani ammunition on Pakistani soldiers.

The pitched battles had become a way of daily life, and by the third day we had captured the township of Shoubara which was twelve kilometres inside Pakistan. All the shops in the deserted bazaar were overflowing with goods. Cash was found lying in the steel cash boxes and the *chullahs* (stoves) of *halwai* (sweet shops) were still burning hot. Stories told to us by the civilians were similar, except that this time they had even been informed by their forces that they were about to reach Delhi.

On the ninth day, the Thillora police station and the Thillora township were captured by us. It was a walled city as there was a thick brick boundary wall all the way around. We found many well-planned fruit gardens there. On that day we also captured a big village which was called Boundial.

On the thirteenth day, the railway line of Pakistan Western Railways from Sialkot to Rawalpindi was destroyed by our unit at Alhar railway station. A few unsold railway tickets were collected by our boys as souvenirs. At that station, a goods train, alongwith a burning steam engine, had been left behind by the Pakistanis.

The next big towns that fell to our forces were known as Dhawinda and Gini Salarian, where highly pitched battles were fought. Hand to hand battles with bayonets were fought during the night before we completely captured both the towns.

On 23 September the ceasefire was declared. We had reached the famous place Hara Peer which was more than thirty kilometres from the original line of control. This town had about 1800 houses, and it was the big food grain market of that area. On the western side of this town was a large mango garden, and at one end there existed an old graveyard.

Our unit was to dig down the bunkers in the graveyard area. We had dug down the channels of trenches which were connected to the bunkers. These bunkers offered us the luxury of office *cum* residence for each officer and a large bunker as the main office. A one hundred yards no man's land separated the opposing armies.

Many a time a desperate enemy soldier would get frustrated and shout why we were sitting on their land. Sometimes, some of our soldiers would shout back, "we have won it." Sometimes a hot atmosphere would emerge out of such exchanges, but our senior officers would bring such situation under control by dialogue. There was no violation of the ceasefire while we were on the enemy land that we had won.

A portion of the bunker which ultimately became my living room was a nicely dug out old grave. It was a nice cool place to live in. I realised why people pray for the peace of the dead.

My immediate senior officer, Captain Raj Kumar, told me that he would come to inspect my bunker. I told my helper about the inspection. He did not spare any effort to clean the bunker, and he deliberately hanged the skeleton of a previous occupant in a corner. It was not possible to make out whether the skeleton belonged to a man or a woman.

When Captain Raj Kumar came into the bunker, he said: "So you have a female companion in your living quarters, without having obtained proper permission? It is against the army rules and good order. You will have to give an explanation for this." In the afternoon, when I was about to enter the officers' mess tent, I was handed over a letter asking for my explanation as to why I had allowed a dead female companion in my living bunker inside the active battle-zone. I was ordered to change over to proper field dress immediately and to report to my commanding officer.

When I saluted and reported to my CO, I was told to go to the rear of our formation HQs to receive a newly-posted officer to our unit. Later on I learnt that the matter of inspection and explanation was a mere field joke.

We stayed in that location for six months, until March 1966. We received orders to hand over all occupied land to Pakistan, fall back to the pre-war borderline, and then move to our earlier peace location.

But many of my close friends, companions and professional colleagues who have laid down their lives still occupy the land that they had won.

2

My War Hero

The experience of my first war in 1965 provided me with a tremendous opportunity to test my ability to lead, to take right initiatives, to make the best of every situation, and to learn never to say die.

In the month of September, when the war broke out, the fully grown up crops of sugarcane and maize presented a tough test of command and control to the field commanders. The high crops gave the soldiers cover of sight but not a shield from the fire. Plain fields provided good roads to army vehicles in all directions. Wherever we drove, our track became a road. Tanks created mayhem because of their high mobility and maneuverability. The infantry, with its power of capturing and physically holding the ground, played the most important role in achieving the victory over an enemy with low morale.

I knew the name of my brigade commander, but I had not yet met him. The first time I met my brigade commander was on the second day of the war (D+1 day). He was called by his nickname "Bally". His full name was Brigadier Balbir Singh Dhillon.

It was in the late afternoon of that day when my company (a force of about one hundred soldiers) was advancing at the left flank of a tank regiment, about seven kilometres inside Pakistani territory. Suddenly I felt a heavy hand on my right shoulder: "Come on, *puttar* (son), keep advancing; I am your Brigade Commander. What the bloody hell."

I noticed a large *sardarji* with brigadier's field-badges on his shoulders. His untidy beard and slightly loose turban showed me that he had been marching for a long time; but I was impressed by his upwards pointing prominent moustache.

"Young man; go ahead and kill the bloody enemy. What the bloody hell ... ? Go, carry on."

I saluted him by bringing my body in an upright position. Then I marched forward. I felt happy to see my brigade commander marching with the assaulting troops. He had left a good impression on me. That raised my confidence.

During the remaining days of the war, he was around most of the time. He would suddenly emerge from nowhere and keep cheering us and pushing us. He would stand on a small mound and roar like a lion. He instantly became my most daring war hero and source of inspiration. What a daredevil! What an Indian!

If I was to say that I enjoyed fighting the war, that would not be a wrong statement, because at that age I had so much enthusiasm and passion that the complete experience seemed like an interesting adventure to me. The war ended on 23 September 1965, on its twentieth day. Our unit had advanced more than thirty kilometres deep into Pakistani territory when the ceasefire was declared. We immediately dug up our defensive positions, wherever we were at the target time of the ceasefire (twelve o'clock midnight) and started to consolidate our positions.

Soon after the ceasefire had commenced, our brigade commander was on an inspection spree, scrutinising all the units under his command. During the inspection, he used to march up to each place of occupation, covering the whole unit-area. He always made a point of talking to the soldiers and young officers.

My unit was inspected about one week after the ceasefire. We had organised a dinner party in our officers' mess to celebrate our victory. Our officers' mess cook, Sepoy Abdul Rahim, was in a great mood. On such occasions, he used to cook his favourite dishes, and nobody could dictate the menu to him. Among the snacks, *reshmi kabab* was one of his favourite dishes. *Reshmi kabab* used to melt as soon as you put it into the mouth, and usually there was a shortage of this dish during every party.

Brigadier Balbir Singh Dhillon was very fond of meat dishes, and he was mightily pleased with the meat preparations. Two bottles of rum were awarded by the brigade commander, who personally handed over the gift to Sepoy Abdul Rahim. My CO announced the promotion of Abdul Rahim to the rank of lance naik.

We had a grand party on that day, dancing and singing. In between the dance sessions I gathered courage and went to my brigade commander. I told him that I was highly impressed by his personal example of guiding the troops at the assault line. I would die on his command, any time, any where.

"Your name is Munnu?" he asked me.

"You know my name, Sir?" I asked.

"Yes, of course I know your name and the names of each one of you, my boy. I am proud of you all. You have all done well. Tell me, how do you feel now, celebrating the victory and dancing on the chest of the enemy? What the bloody hell."

"We all are very proud of you, sir," I said.

"Proud of me? Why, what for? I have never fired even a single shot. Why are you proud of me? You people fought the war and have won it. The whole credit must go to you all. You, my boys, taught them a lesson. What the bloody hell ... these ... ." He added some adjectives in punjabi language and then turned to shake hands with me; then he told me, "come and see me in my office tomorrow at 10:00 a.m. Right, Rolly?" he looked at my CO.

"Yes, sir," my CO replied to his Commander.

On the next day I reported to my brigade commander at 10:00 a.m. Two cups of tea were served to us as soon as he had gestured to me to sit down on a chair.

He said, "young man, I would have had a son of your age, had I married."

"You remained a bachelor, sir? What happened? Why didn't you marry, sir?" I asked.

"Why didn't I marry? Yea, that is a good question. Why did you not marry, Brigadier Bally? What the bloody hell … .Yes, it is a good question. Ah … do you really want to know, son?" my Commander asked me.

"Yes, sir, I really want to know why you did not marry. Please do tell me!" I replied.

"Oh, that is a long story … a long old story. You see, when I was young man like you, I fell in love with a girl whose name was Prabhjot. We loved each other very much. We were classmates. My people were rich farmers, and Prabhjot's father was our *kastakar*, in a village in the Hoshiarpur district of Punjab. You know what a Kastakar is? *Kastakars* were landless people who used to till our land for their living.

"We used to meet everyday. We had promised to marry each other, when the right time came. But the right time never came. Do you know what happened? No, how would you know what had happened? Okay, I will tell you. You see, my people came to know about the affair, and they strongly objected to such a relationship. I was told not to meet her any more.

"But I was very firm – adamant, you can say. I told my *bapu* (father) that I will certainly marry her. I refused to take meals. I remained without food for two days. What the bloody hell … a hunger strike for the sake of love. Have you ever heard of such a thing?

"Any way, my parents relented, and they agreed to the marriage on the condition that it would be celebrated at the right age. I also agreed. Prabhjot and I started meeting again. Obviously, her parents had also agreed. Thus, nearly one year passed. Prabhjot was not very good at her studies. Tuition was arranged for her in a teacher's house. I used to drop her at her tutor's place on my motor-bike, and bring her back, every day. This went on for about eight months.

"One day we were shocked to find that both the teacher and Prabhjot had fled the town where we used to live. All efforts to trace them were futile. I could not imagine that Prabhjot could ditch me and could run away with someone else. I felt cheated by the one who was closest to me. It was difficult, very difficult, for me.

"I was the only son of my parents. They were badly hurt and highly agitated. The first outburst of my father was to throw her parents from our land. I intervened and persuaded him not to take such action because it was not their fault. I, too, had a spell of depression and used to keep to myself, most of the time trying to make out why it had to happen to me. My father decided to send me for higher studies to my maternal uncle, who lived in Jammu. My maternal uncle had a son of my age. His name was Tajender Singh Gill.

"Tajender turned out to be my saviour. Jammu is not far away from the Pakistan border, and many times Tajender took me to border villages, like Kahnachack and Akhnoor, which were situated on the banks of the River Chenab; very fast streams of ice-cold water flowed out of that river.

"Tajender told me the stories of great legends, such as those of Sohni-Mahiwal, Mirza-Sahiban and Heer-Ranjha. They are the most interesting love stories, and they were very popular in those days. They had all lived on the banks of the River Chenab. People still sang the sweetest songs about the tragic love stories of those people. They had all sacrificed their lives for the sake of their love.

"There was a saying in that area that once in a year the colour of the water that flows in the Chenab becomes mud brown when the river used to overflow in rainy season. People used to say that the blood of those lovers mixed with the water flowed during that time and thus swelled the river. I found a lot of peace sitting on the banks of the great River Chenab and watching the uncontrollable roar of the waves, which was similar to what was going on inside me.

"Tajender was preparing for the examination for joining the armed forces and for the interview by the Services Selection Board. He advised me to do the same thing and inspired me to invest all my energies into giving my love to the real beloved, our motherland, which never betrays. We were both selected and joined the army.

"Later on, I learnt that Prabhjot and the professor had returned to their house, with a baby boy, after about two years. There was a lot of commotion and anger in the families. I had to prevail upon my people and on her parents to ignore the issue, because nothing could be undone. Ah, this is my story. That is the reason why I have remained unmarried. How could one get married after being betrayed so badly, as I was?

"Now you know as to why I have not married. The unfaithful woman and a foolish man like me, a total idiot of a man, who used to take his beloved to her lover and bring her back to leave her at her house, every day. What a stupid fool was made of you, Brigadier Bally."

I was spellbound and did not know what to say. For a while I could not utter a word. Then I suddenly said: "I am sorry, I am really very sorry, sir."

"What for, what have you done?" he asked.

"Not me, I didn't do anything to you, but my mother did."

"What, what the bloody hell ... you are Prabhjot's son? Oh my God; and you kept listening to me, whatever rubbish I said. Oh *puttar*, please forgive me, please forgive me, my son."

He took me in his arms...almost wrapped me in his embrace...My real war hero.

3

Love Without Response Has No Life

My first encounter with Sakkhi took place during a friendly cricket match, which was being played for the entertainment of soldiers between the Indian team and 'J and K State Eleven' at the Bakshi stadium in Jammu. I noticed a young lady sitting two rows ahead of me in the officers' enclosure; she was greatly enjoying the match by making a loud noise of clapping and shouting at every shot.

I was fascinated by her vibrant features, her bold dress, and her carefree modern hairdo. I could not help shouting in high pitch, although my shouts were not actually meant for the good shots, but were intended to attract her attention. She looked back quite generously, every time when I shouted high to back up the batsman, she flashed a wide smile at me.

Did this mean that we had some thing common? Some of the officers who were sitting in the same enclosure made grinning gestures at me, as if I was acting cheaply to attract her attention. But who cared? Did the grins of the officers mean that they were also bowled over by her beauty? Or were they just jealous of the smiles which she directed towards me?

I felt that life should also be treated like a cricket match. Make a loud noise when you hit well, and say a loud 'Oh no' when you are bowled over. Try to create excitement on every occasion, and never let your spirits go deep down, because otherwise the stresses and strains would ride on you and make you lose the match.

Honestly, by the end of the day I had forgotten which team had lost or won the match, but I knew very well that I had lost something very precious to her.

From then on, I became very keen to discover where she lived. I was lucky to get some information about her from a close friend of mine who told me that she was the widow of an army officer who had sacrificed his life in the last war. Hence, she was always made a special invitee in most of the functions that were held in the formation headquarters.

I felt deep anguish about her fate and tried to put the entire blame on God, the almighty, who had created such a lovely and cheerful human being and then forced all the miseries of life upon her. At such a prime age, she had been burdened with all the sadness that nature had in its store.

But on second thoughts I realised that she did not look sad at all. Maybe she had never loved her husband and did not feel any pain for losing him. I got confused whether I was agitated against God for her misfortune or whether I was trying to blame her for being unfaithful to her late husband. Such thoughts further nourished my eagerness to meet her as early as possible. I made sure that I obtained an entry to the next get-together at which she was an invitee.

As soon as the first opportunity presented itself to me, I approached her and said, "do you remember me? The cricket match ... and the loud noise .... I really enjoyed the strokes very well. Oh, it was a very thrilling match."

"How could anybody forget the biggest cause of distraction?" she taunted me casually.

"Distraction, to attract attention .... Do you mean that? At least I felt the same way about you. But let me assure you, madam, that your beauty was a bigger distraction to the crowd than my noise," I said.

"Is that a compliment for me or an attempt to justify yourself?" she asked.

"Of course it is a sincere and true compliment for you. At least I was completely bowled over by your enchanting smile and graceful body, and I must convey my hearty thanks and gratitude to you for looking back, occasionally." I added.

"You sound quite interesting. What do you want from me?" Had she guessed my intentions?

"Friendship, of course. You have correctly guessed that I am attracted to you with a sincere mind," I tried to assure her.

"Why do you use word sincerely again and again? Don't you have any confidence in yourself or in the language which you speak?" she asked.

"On the contrary, I am completely confident that I too have impressed you and that we can be good friends," I said.

"Do you really think so?" she asked me.

"Yea, surely. Please accept my invitation to be a close friend of mine. You will always feel happy about making that decision. I can assure you of that," I added with all the emphasis of my body language to convince her.

She extended her hand, and I grabbed it hurriedly and said, "Thanks a million."

"What next?" she asked

"When are we meeting again?" I had a readymade question.

"Ah ... okay; let me think it over .... Okay, be my guest for lunch in my house next Sunday. Tell me about one of your favourite dishes that I can cook for you," she said.

"You are very generous and kind. I will be there at 12:00 noon. It shows that you like cooking. Oh, I love the homely ladies. My favourite dish is red-beans curry," I said.

"How many women are there in your life? And please make it 2:00 p.m. I get up late in the morning," she said

"Only two, my mother and my elder sister. And now you are the third one. I will be with you at 2:00 p.m. sharp. Thanks," I added before she excused herself to talk to someone else.

I was very excited but could not avoid a doubt rising in my mind. What had made her extend such an intimate invitation to me so easily, without even knowing me well? I presumed that there might be a function at her house already arranged and she might have invited me as an additional guest. Or was she that easily available?" I could not find an answer.

I turned up at her house at the exact time with a large bouquet of flowers which consisted mainly of red roses.

She received me with a broad, cordial smile. "I love red roses. How did you know that? Thanks." She led me to an empty and well-decorated sitting room.

"You have a great taste in interior decoration. Where are the other guests?" I asked her.

"There is nobody else. You wanted to be a close friend, so there is no question of others between close friends. Why, had you wanted to meet me in a crowd?" she asked.

"No, but I thought you wouldn't put blind faith in someone without even knowing him well," I managed to say.

"Yes, you are right. I have made some inquiries about you, and I was told that you are a gentleman, though one who is slightly more emotional than other guys," she replied.

"Is that a shortcoming?" I asked.

"No. Had I considered that a shortcoming, I would not have invited you to my house," she said.

I said, "pardon me for saying this, but since we have now accepted each other as close friends, let us be frank and free with each other on all matters."

"What do you mean by that?" she asked.

"I mean that we are justified to find out some details about each other's past, so that we can start the relationship with clear mind," I said.

"What clarification do you need from me?" she asked me.

"Oh, no clarification, please. But I was just thinking that, from your present lifestyle one gets to presume that you did not love your late husband. Or may be you have understood the realities of life so soon and have adjusted yourself." I added.

"Your first assumption is wrong. Ours was a love marriage. I loved him very much when he was alive. But now, when he is no more - nowhere to see or to feel or to respond - what do I do? To whom do I express my love? Love without response has no life. There are only two ways to live without him: either keep on mourning and expressing my miseries to every one, or accept the realties of life, and restart living in a normal way. Which, do you think, is the way for me? If I have to live, and if there is no choice but to breathe on this earth, do I have any right to the fresh air or not? Tell me what is right for me?" She sounded quite angry with me.

I had no option but to express regret for my mistake. "I feel very sorry for my big blunder and wrong assumption. I apologise sincerely and will never again let my mind be misguided by such useless thoughts. Please forgive me."

Hesitantly, I bent forward and held her hand, which she allowed me to hold for some time, and said, "I thought that you were somewhat different from other people. Others may also be thinking the same way about me. Don't you realise that I am a victim, not an offender?"

I saw two pearls of purest water roll down her cheeks. I felt like washing my soul with those two drops, but I did not dare touch her again.

I tried to continue the conversation, "Tell me what are you going to do with your life? I mean, what are your plans for your life in the future? And could I be of any help any time?"

"Not yet planned. In fact, I have decided not to plan anything. What is the future? Where is the future? Who has seen tomorrow? I planned to settle down once and see where I have ended up. I do not know where the end is?" she replied.

"Every end, in itself, is a start for something else. It is for us to realise this as early as possible, so that we can welcome and adopt the new. I sincerely wish that you take me as one of the points of your restart," I said.

"I don't know what are you hinting at?" she said

"Let me explain. The few moments that we have lived together are a good basis for the start of our friendship. I am sure that we are very close to agreeing that our views are similar and that we can be equally helpful to each in discarding our tragic past and face the coming time together."

"I am not ready for re-marriage. Are you trying to propose to me?" she asked.

"No. That is too early to say now. We have to understand each other first and take the decision when the right time comes." I clarified.

"You mentioned about your tragic past. Tell me: What happened?" She was keen to know.

"I lost my first love in an air crash. Please forgive me for not going into details. You rightly said that there is no use in trying to relive a past that can nowhere be seen or felt. Let us agree on that. I think it would be a good idea to try the food. Have you cooked red beans? I am starving. Can we have food, Sakkhi?"

"Oh yes. Why not, give me two minutes," she left for the kitchen. I followed her and offered to carry the dishes to the table.

All the dishes that she had prepared had the touch of a good cook. She insisted to put food in my plate. I found that she felt satisfaction in feeding me first and then eating herself. She was a very poor eater.

My mind was working faster than the speed of eating the food. I was feeling discomfort and was not able to find the right words to make a suggestion for the next meeting to her. I did not want 'no' as an answer, so I was trying to put it in an acceptable way.

"What is still bothering you? Why, do you need any other clarification?" she said.

"Oh, please, for God's sake, do not embarrass me any more by making me realise my earlier mistake. I have already apologised. Honestly, I was just thinking as to how to invite you for dinner or another programme?"

"Just say, 'would you join me this evening for dinner; madam?' and I would say 'yes, sir, with great pleasure." She changed the serious environment with a touch of child-like acting. I repeated what she said.

Our dinner meeting was splendid, and our subsequent meetings were splendid, too. The more we met, the more we discovered ourselves. Our eagerness to know more about each other was boundless. The closer we came, the more we realised how little we knew each other, and from that came our craving to meet again.

It is very strange that the more you know about a subject, the more you realise that there is still a lot more to be learnt than what you knew before. The true knowledge keeps your hunger always unsatisfied.

"Eh, you have become serious again. Please wake up and be with me. Can I do any thing for you?" she asked.

"Oh no, absolutely nothing, please. In fact, I must say that you are a so relaxed, easy and cool person that nobody could feel uncomfortable with you. I was just thinking why God has been so cruel to you?" I said.

"Please shut up, will you? Do not start talking again about a subject which we have already settled. I feel so lucky now that God has sent you my way. Let me play some soothing music for you." She got up and played my favourite *ghazal*, sung by the old legend Begum Akhtar,

"*Hazaron khawashen aisy, ki har khawahish per dum nikkle,*

Bahut nikkle mere arman, magar phir bhi kam nikkle."

(The desires which I have in my mind are so numerous and every desire is more interesting than the other. God has fulfilled many of my wishes but there are still many more.)

And now, after more than three decades of living together we are discovering new facts about life. Our lives, which were dragging on emptily before we had met, suddenly picked up such a high speed that we did not quite realise that the people had already started calling us senior citizens.

Today our children are married and well-settled. It is strange that when we try to teach them how to handle their kids, we realise that there were always better ways for us of bringing them up.

Another thing that I have realised now is that our love has grown up with the passage of time. We have now developed a mature outlook on life. Life is no longer like a cricket match now. The craving for excitement has disappeared. We care for each other much more than ever before. But I think that Sakkhi has not changed much. The only small change that I see in her is that she has now become somewhat critical of certain habits of mine. She has drifted into a tendency of reminding me what to eat and what not to eat, and has started to give me instructions like a grandmother – to get up early, and to go for regular walks, everyday. She insists on doing everything for me, and she does not like anybody else – not even my daughter-in-law – to serve food to me. I also feel better to be dependent on her, much more than ever before. Her habit of serving me food on a plate has not changed.

The chariot of life is travelling with constant speed, and the routine is all set for similar activities everyday. We do not care for the excitements anymore, and we feel contented in tolerating each other in a natural manner. Nature has started its process of aging our bodies.

Unconsciously, we are prepared to welcome the end, because every end is a beginning of something new.

4

Love of Three Generations

Soon after the capture of the village Dharwa, during 1965 war, on the first day of the attack, I was informed by my immediate subordinate that two enemies were still hiding in a small mud house. After reaching the wall of the house, I found a very old, lean and thin man was peeping out of a small window. Seeing me with a pistol in my hand he signalled to me to go near him and said, "Please kill me and my sick wife."

I asked, "Who else is there inside the room?"

"Nobody; they all have run away, leaving us to die. But nobody is killing us, not even nature," said the old man.

I went inside the room and found that an equally old and frail woman was lying on the broken bed with the fear of death on her face. She looked very sick, with her wide-open eyes that looked very prominent and unusually big on her wrinkled face.

She said, "Don't kill me. Give me some water."

Instantly, I uncorked my water bottle and put it to her lips. She was very thirsty and drank nearly half of the water in the bottle. She was breathing heavily. Then, suddenly, she started crying bitterly. I felt that almost an equal amount of water must have rolled down from her eyes. I looked at the old man. The old man signalled to me to leave her alone. I left the bottle by her side and came out of the room. My companion officer asked me whether he should shoot them.

"No, leave them. They will die a natural death in a day or two anyway," I told him; and we marched on to join our other colleagues.

The heat of war was on its peak. I had forgotten all about the old couple. After twenty days of hectic war, the ceasefire was declared, and both the armies halted wherever they were to take defensive positions. We reorganised ourselves and consolidated our defences.

A few days later, I was told to go to our 'Rear HQs' for a job, and I had to cross that village. On reaching the place, I found smoke coming out from one of the houses. Soon I realised that the smoke was emerging from the same house where we had left the old couple.

I told my driver to halt and shouted, "Who is there?"

The same old man came out and looked at me closely, "Oh, you have come to take your water bottle back. Anyway, we do not need it any more. Please take it with you." He went inside to search for it.

I said, "Please don't bother. I have another one. Tell me how did you survive all these days?"

"Oh, another '*Farishta*' (god) like you came and did not let us die. In any case, my wife refuses to die, as she believes that her sons would come back one day. I do not know why she is holding on. I think it is our time to go now. We have seen enough of life: Ample love, immense hatred and destruction of war. What else do you find in the drama of life? Everything that a normal human being would like to go through in one life has been our destiny. What more is there for us now? She is living in a dreamland and insists on seeing her granddaughter get married. Tell me, how is that possible?" I realised that the old man had wanted someone to talk to for long time.

I went inside and asked the old woman, "How are you feeling now?"

"I am okay. He accuses me of clinging on to life. But tell me, how can one die without paying back one's debts? Our religion teaches us that, if you owe something to someone, you must pay back your debts in this life only. We owe our lives to the young man. And apart from that we have some obligations to fulfil. I must get my granddaughter married to him. He loves her so much. Before the war, when my granddaughter was with us, she had confided in me that she too loved him immensely. Tell me how I can die before fulfilling my duties?" The old woman also had a lot to talk.

On her insistence, I sat down on another cot, remained there and asked, "Who is this man to whom you want your granddaughter to get married?"

"He is from across the border. A man from your country, Hindustan. But how does that matter? How do the boundaries matter to real lovers? He is a man, after all - a good human being. He took a grave risk to save us during the war. He fed us and looked after us like his own parents. He brought us food, clothes and medicines when our own people had left us to die starving. I want him and my granddaughter to be united. Can you help us?" asked the old woman.

"No, I cannot. Who is this man? Where does he live?" I asked.

She said, "How can I tell you when you ask like that? Would you arrest him?"

"No, why should I arrest him? I do not think that he has committed any crime by giving you food and medicines," I replied.

"You seem to be a man of wisdom. I must confide in you. Look how history repeats itself. You see, nearly twenty five years ago, his maternal aunt, who lived across the border, ran away from her house and came to us to get married to my younger son. We arranged their marriage immediately, before there could be any objection from her people or the government. They too loved each other very much at that time. They have been a loving couple until now. Now, if these youngsters love each other so much, what is wrong? After all, loving someone is not a crime. You ask this old man. What did he do to me when he was young? Ask him," She tried to insist. I looked at the old man.

He looked embarrassed, but said, "Why waste the time of a generous man. You may proceed on your way, sir. Do not listen to this stupid old lady."

"How am I stupid? You are a stupid, old, dirty man. How many days ago you had a bath? Tell me, honestly. Do you ever listen to what I say? He always keeps discouraging me," she shot back at him.

I was amused by their behaviour. They behaved like a newly-wed couple. And I asked the old man, "Tell me, what you did you do to her when she was young?"

Before he could reply, she spoke again, "Did you notice a blush in his eyes. It must have reminded him of the good old days. The poor old man: I pity him. Let me assure you that he would not be able to tell you anything. I will tell you. You see, when I was young, he entangled me in his love and made me pregnant and cross the border and run away with him. Oh, there was big commotion all over, but we survived. Now we laugh when old memories are revived. Those were the real days. And now, when I tell him that we must try to settle our granddaughter with the young man, he feels unsure of himself. I do not know why the power of anyone's spirit should diminish with the advance of age. The spirit does not get old. Religion says 'it never dies.' I do not know what is happening to this man. Age is eating him up ... ." Perhaps she wanted to continue talking, but I was getting late for my assignment; so I took leave from them and proceeded on my journey.

After about three months, I happened to cross the same village again. And I thought of meeting the old couple. When I reached the house, I found that it was closed. Thinking that the young man might have taken them with him to his village, I proceeded further. At the end of that village, there was a mango grove. I found a young man sitting under a tree, crying bitterly.

I asked him about the cause of his misery and he narrated to me that the old couple had died the previous night - and he had given them a burial, just a little while ago. On asking the cause of their death, he told me that the previous evening when he came to meet them, both were in their usual good health. But he himself was sad because he had heard that their granddaughter whom he loved and wanted to marry had already been married to someone else by her parents.

After that, he left them - only to be informed the next morning that both of them had died in their sleep.

5

Love Affairs of Some Enemy Soldiers

Soon after midnight, when the ceasefire had become effective, our first priority was to dig down the fire trenches and bunkers along the line of control. Our CO had indicated to us the general area of deployment, and we decided our platoon and company layout according to the topography.

Early the next morning I was called by my CO. My second-in-command was also with him. The CO said, "I want to assign a special duty to you. I think that the enemy has left approximately twenty dead bodies, which are scattered within our unit area. I presume that all of them were Mohammedan by religion. They will be given burial. You have a Muslim JCO by the name of Subedar Khuda Baksh in your company. Brief him of this duty. Pick up ten other Mohammedan boys to help him. Remember that the dead bodies belonged to the soldiers. Now they no longer exist as our enemies. Tell your boys not to mishandle them, and just give them a burial. Also ensure that there is no fanfare whatsoever. 2-I-C will allot the area for the graveyard. You must begin immediately, because – for medical reasons - no delay can be permitted. Get help from the RMO (regimental medical officer), if necessary.

There are two very important points. Firstly, if you find anybody still alive, hand him over to the doctor immediately, for treatment. Secondly, if you find any documents on them, or if you discover any other worthwhile information, inform the 2-I-C. He will directly supervise the efforts. If there are no questions, you can leave now."

I called Subedar Khuda Baksh and ten other Mohammedan troops and briefed them properly. The job was completed by the late afternoon. I gave the completion report to my 2-I-C.

Early the next morning, I was informed by the in-charge of the night patrol that he had noticed some flowers lying on one of the graves during the night.

I proceeded to the place immediately with the informer. On reaching the spot I did not find any flowers on the grave, but a little distance away I found a small bunch of flowers lying near a bush. Someone had probably removed them before anybody could notice.

Did that amount to the fanfare, such as the old man was referring to, and was that a disciplinary case?

I immediately called all the individuals concerned and asked them who had done that. Initially all of them kept quiet, but after some time, Subedar Khuda Baksh admitted that he had placed the flowers on that specific grave. I dismissed the others.

I asked the JCO, "Tell me *sahib*, why did you offer flowers to the dead body of the enemy, and whose grave is that?"

He replied, "Sir, the dead soldier was my sister's son?"

"How do you know that?" I asked.

"It was during the search for documents that I found a letter in his pocket," he replied.

"A letter? What sort of letter? What was written in that letter?" I asked.

"Sir, he had written the letter to my daughter," he replied.

"To your daughter?" I asked.

"Yes, he was engaged to her three years ago and has been writing to her since then," the JCO replied.

"Have you handed over that letter along with the other letters and articles which you have found?" I asked.

"No, sir, it was my daughter's personal letter," he said.

"You should now hand over that letter as a proof of what you say. In any case, no one knows that the letter was written to your daughter," I told him.

And so he handed over the letter. I reported the whole matter to my CO, saying, "Sir, Subedar Khuda Baksh has not disobeyed any orders, because there was no fanfare involved. Fanfare means conspicuous display of joy or any other kind of celebrations which are meant to be seen by other people. In this case the JCO has paid homage to his close relative quietly, without any intention of anybody else coming to know about his feelings. He also made a point of ensuring that the homage offered was not to be seen by any one. I recommend that no action should be taken against him. He is a good JCO, sir."

My CO said, "You talk too much. Speak when you are spoken to. Did I say that I was going to take any action against the JCO? Do I have to learn military law from you? I know that you are trying to shield your JCO. But you are trying to teach me how to command my troops. Now, since you have started the topic, I instruct you to check, and prepare a list of, all the articles and documents which were found on the dead bodies. They may provide some worthwhile information. Put up your detailed assessment and report the completion to me by ten hundred hours tomorrow morning."

I saluted my CO and got on with the job, which entailed working late into night to complete the task within the given time. I submitted the completion report in time.

During the scrutiny, I found some very interesting letters. Several poignant portions from some of those letters are quoted in succeeding paragraphs.

1. **One of the letters contained nice poetry in Urdu, which meant something like this:**
   "The blue sky above me is full of clouds.
   These clouds are different from those
   that shower the water in the fields.
   These clouds are born out of the dust and dirt,
   That rises due to the thumping of heavy boots of the clashing enemies,
   The enemies with deadly weapons,
   The weapons, those are used for killing and destruction of life of humans.
   I will kill the enemy,
   the real enemy who created hatred among the human beings."

2. **Another letter, which also contained poetry and was addressed to someone's mother, read:**
   "Mother, oh my dear mother,
   Why didn't you give birth to me in some other part of the world?
   In the peaceful parts like North Pole or perhaps the South Pole,
   Where every thing is cool – very, very cool.
   And I wish that you had lived in the warm water,
   Under the thick layer of frozen ice.
   I wish that you were a fish, a big fish like a whale,
   That would hide me under her huge belly,
   And save me from deadly sharks."

3. **There was a letter, probably from a young beloved of a soldier, which read somewhat like this:**
   "My love, my life, …
   "You came like the strong wind of summer,
   which comes whirling around and taking away,

The heat and dust towards the sky,
That converts into clouds, pregnant with water,
The thick beautiful black clouds,
When they become very heavy and cannot hold the yield any more,
They start poring on my ground and everywhere around,
And make the earth wet and fertile to give new life to nature,
I saw that happening in the seasons that have come and that have gone,
But this time it is different, absolutely different,
The clouds are not beautiful because they are thin and white,
They are like barren earth, hard and dry,
That is how I feel now,
Under the feet of dirty boots of the advancing enemy."

4. **In another letter one soldier had written to his wife:**

"My dear Hussaina,

"My seniors say that we should treat our personal weapon (rifle) like our wife. And so I am doing that, holding it with the tight grip, in my hands. Do not try to slip away, and I really mean it. In my absence, don't ever flirt with anybody else. Don't laugh with your big mouth wide open, as you normally do, when outsiders are present.

"I don't like that. And I will not tolerate it at all. You know how badly I treat the women. If I find you doing anything like that, I will kill you when I come back, if I come back ... ."

5. **Another letter that was found on the body of a dead soldier read thus:**

"My love, my life, my dear;

"You have gone away and taken with you all the sources of my peace and solace. I feel worse than a fish that has been taken out of the water and thrown on the burning hot sand of a widespread desert. I know that there is no getting out of this horrible situation. I told you not to leave me behind. I have repeatedly tried to make you understand the bad intentions of your friend, for whom you have left me and whom you have trusted the most. I do not understand why you did not have faith in me, and had more faith on the most unworthy kind of a friend.

"Now everything is finished. The greatest gift that a woman can offer to her man on their wedding day has been snatched away from me. I have nothing to offer to you now. I have been completely ruined. There is no use in my living now. I hate my body. It gives me a foul smell of rotten flesh. I cannot tolerate the weight of my body on my soul. So I have decided to kill myself. By the time you receive my letter, I will be breathing no more. It is final. Do not take any chances.

"You know that our love was based on the mutual trust of pious sentiments. I was pure like the untouchable body of the sun. But now the sun has been eclipsed.

"I know that you also cannot live without me, and would certainly like to take the revenge. But you don't have to make your hands dirty with his impure blood. I have already done that. I have killed the brute culprit.

"And if you find life unbearable, rather die fighting the enemy on the battlefield. I will wait for you in the next life.

"Till then, *khuda hafiz* ... .
Naheed"

6

One Life Is Not Enough for Love

After the war, we decided to make our headquarters at Sabazpeer. It was located more than thirty-five kilometres from the old line of control, deep inside Pakistan. We consolidated our defences there. A network of trenches was laid out in such a way that every bunker was interconnected. One could easily walk from one bunker to another without being observed on the surface of the territory.

Security arrangements of a very high standard were made. Vigilance during day and night was maintained by sentries who were regularly checked by the officers on duty, all around the clock. It was never forgotten that we were deep inside enemy territory.

On one early morning, at about 4:30 a.m., we were alarmed by enemy firing. Our troops returned fire at once, and then followed a heavy exchange of fire. We all took our positions immediately.

I heard a loud cry and assumed that someone, very close to and in front of my company location, was hit by a bullet. Since nobody from our side had gone forward, I guessed that it was one of the enemies. If my assumption was correct, the enemy would have come very close to our position. I immediately started crawling towards the sound. After coming within about thirty yards of the figure, I found a woman was lying in a pool of blood. She raised her hands and said, "don't shoot. I am a friend." And she collapsed. I observed that there was nobody else nearby.

I crawled under the ceiling of fire and started dragging the woman towards our position. Other boys helped me in bringing the woman inside the bunker.

The bullet had pierced the leg of the woman. First aid was given to her, and she was immediately brought to the field ambulance medical unit for treatment at our rear location. After some time, firing from the enemy side stopped, and a white flag came up. This meant that they were requesting for a ceasefire.

The woman became the topic of the day. Why would a beautiful and modern young girl want to cross the heavily guarded border? Everyone began to speculate who she was and why she had tried to cross the border in such a way. Some people said that she was a Pakistani spy. But why was she shot at if she was their intelligence agent? Maybe it was the trick of the enemy to induct their hardcore agent in a way which would make the Indian army believe that she was simply a defector.

They did shoot at her. But why she was shot in the leg? Was she shot in the leg on purpose or had the shooter aimed poorly? The vigilance experts were discussing many such questions. They questioned her repeatedly. In the hospital she was operated upon to remove the bullet from her thigh-bone.

After a few days, I was told to accompany certain officers from the military intelligence wing to meet her. I was instructed to talk to her while others listened and watched. I memorised a set of questions. On reaching the hospital, I was introduced to her.

She said, "I am told that you saved my life, braving a hail of bullets. Why did you do that, officer?"

"Initially I just wanted to find exactly how many enemies have crept into my area, but on finding that you, a lonely woman, lying in the pool of blood, but still alive, it became my duty to save you," I replied.

"Even though I was a stranger?" she asked.

"Yes, even though you were a stranger," I replied.

"You Indians can risk of your lives to save even the strangers from enemy land. Good, too good. Brave officer, I owe my life to you, lucky man," she said.

"Why am I lucky?" I asked

"Because, God has given you the privilege to save the life of a human being. God has selected you to perform that noble task; that is why you are lucky," she replied.

"You are very religious," I said.

"Yes, everybody should be religious, and grateful to God, because He has granted us a beautiful life and a purpose."

"Purpose?" I asked.

"Yes, haven't you studied Geeta and the theory of Karma? The purpose is Karma which means good deeds and that even accompanies you into the next life according to your own religion," she said

"Have you read Geeta? Do you have Geeta in your country?" I asked.

"Yes, why not? We must adopt what is good and virtuous from anyone, anytime. I have done a masters degree in English literature and doctorate in Religious Studies," she replied.

"You are highly qualified," I said.

"Degrees are not important; it is the knowledge that matters. I have left all my degrees in the country from which I have defected."

"What has made you defect from your country?" I asked.

"There are many reasons. Leave that for your intelligence wing to discover," she replied

"So you have prepared yourself for a grilling. Who trained you? ISI?" I asked.

"I have nothing to do with ISI. When I decided to defect I knew I would have to face the vigilance. I knew you people would never believe me otherwise. I left all my people in their country."

"Their country?" I asked.

"Yes, what I have left for good does not belong to me anymore. I live in the present, not the past. What about you?" she asked.

I said, "My life started twenty six years ago. The past is my proud possession. I live my today to improve upon my deeds of yesterday."

"Excellent, your reply is relevant and a most fitting answer to the question. It is marvellous. I have never met an intelligent man like you ... and handsome too," she said.

"Thanks, but I want to know your background," I said.

"Certainly, I know that you would like to know my background, and you have all the right to know it, especially since you gave me new lease of life. I will tell you everything in detail – but, I think, may be not here, in this hospital ... maybe some time later."

"No, I cannot control my curiosity; please tell me every thing now," I asked.

"My name is Rukhsana. I lived with my mother and a younger sister in Lahore. My father was a doctor. He died four years ago. My mother is a teacher in a girls' higher secondary school. I told you about my qualifications. In fact, I was looking for a job as a lecturer in a college when circumstances compelled me to take this step."

"What circumstances?" I asked.

"You are too inquisitive. Please give me some more time," she said.

"Time for what? For making a story?" I asked.

"No, I have not risked my life for making a story, but to live my life the way I want," she said.

"And how do you think that you can live your life the way you want in a country which you have entered illegally?" I asked.

"The logic that you should understand is that the people who have tried to kill me and who have prevented me from entering this country are my enemies, and they take me as their enemy too; that is why they have tried to kill me. You people have no legal way to grant citizenship to the people of that country. I thought that I would cross the border and just mingle among you people, because we all look alike and speak a common language. Apart from that, I have many relatives in India who can support me. I am sure that the Pakistani army people will presume me to be dead."

"What if they find out that you are still alive?" I asked

"How can they find out?" she asked.

"Vigilance," I said.

"Do you think their vigilance is so strong that it can break through your security?" she asked.

"Never take your enemy lightly. And remember that you are the captive of the Indian army. Tell everything correctly. We will verify each detail that you give to us. Anyway, I will move on. Someone is waiting for me," I warned her.

"Your wife?"

"No, I am unmarried. My helper, Sepoy Sher Singh," I replied.

"Oh, you are so mindful of the time of your servant," she said.

"He is not my servant. He is a respected soldier of the Indian army." I was angry with her.

"Sorry, sir. I salute you and your honourable soldier. When shall we meet again?" she asked.

"Never. Why should I meet you again?" I sounded annoyed.

"And if I want to meet you?" she asked.

"No, that is not possible. But why do you want to meet me again?" I asked.

"I have not even thanked you enough. I must meet you again. My religion teaches me not to be ungrateful. Please, for God's sake, let me meet you again, sir," she pleaded.

I did not say anything and left. Soon I got busy in my official affairs, but she kept haunting me. I could not accept her version that she had defected because she wanted to live her life her way. It was not plausible. Her other explanation - that circumstances had forced her to take such dangerous step - also was not convincing at all. There were many unanswered questions. Nobody knew anything, and we thought that it would be better to wait for the investigations to be completed.

After a few days, I received a letter from her. She had written, "my dear saviour, may you be blessed with all happiness. Please forgive me for writing this letter to you. I only hope it will not cause you any inconvenience or embarrassment. My purpose to write this letter to you is that I have no past and that my future is most uncertain. My present is full of misery, unhappiness and loneliness.

"Everyday I am being put through tough grilling sessions. I have told them everything truthfully. But they are not satisfied. They want more information. They are also right, as they are doing their duty. They have to satisfy themselves. Sometimes I feel guilty. I have put so many people in thick soup. My mother and my sister will also face a very bad situation.

"I have given them the addresses of my relatives in India. None of my relatives has visited me so far. Perhaps they are scared. My grandmother is in India. And my real maternal uncle, and so many other close relatives, are also in India. But none of them has come so far.

"I had thought that once I have crossed the border, all my problems would be sorted out. But I feel that my problems are increasing every day. In fact, I feel bad and even ashamed of myself for what I have done. I have no right to bother you. You have been good to me; hence I should make sure that I do not cause even the slightest hassle to you.

"I feel that I have committed a grave mistake and must face the music. But I do not know for how long. I don't think that I deserve this. I wish that the enemy bullet would have killed me. I really wish now that you would have left me to bleed to death. But what can a human being do. Whatever happens in this world happens according to God's wish. If we have to suffer, we cannot help it, and we definitely will suffer.

"My purpose of writing you this letter is only my own satisfaction. At first I thought that I will write to you only one big word of thanks. But I cannot stop writing - you are the one and only human being on this earth, today, with whom I have some connection, merely on humanitarian grounds, because you saved my life. My only prayers to God are that He grants me an opportunity to do something for you, anything.

I have a feeling that they will soon move me from here to some secret place. You need not reply to my letter if you think that I have become a cause of embarrassment to you. Please, for God's sake, please forgive me - forgive me, please. How I crave to see you sometime, just to know that you have forgiven me.

"*Nikaal to laye the, tum hamari kashti toofan se,*
Lakin kinare pe aake, jane kahan kho gai?"
(You have saved me from the storms and have brought my boat to the riverbank. But where did you disappear to after saving me?")

"Yours, indebted for ever,
Rukhsana"

I went straight to my commanding officer to show him the letter. He was in a meeting, but as soon as he learnt that I have come to meet him, he called me inside. I gave the letter to my CO and told him that I had just received it from her.

My CO made me sit on the chair. He gave me a copy of that letter and told that he had already read the letter and was discussing it with the officers from the intelligence wing.

A senior officer from intelligence wing asked me, "Do you want to meet her?"

"No. What makes you ask that?" I asked.

"Nothing in particular, but she wants to meet you urgently," he said.

"She told me that earlier also, in the hospital, and you know that I have refused her," I said.

"Okay, but if we ask you to meet her?" he asked.

"Is that a suggestion or an order?" I asked.

"Yes, maybe it is an order," he said.

"How can I disobey an order?" I replied.

My CO intervened. "Look, Major Paawan, the investigations so far have not revealed much, but our doubts have been nourished further."

"What doubts?" I asked.

"Doubts that she has some links with ISI. Her story that she has defected from her country for the sake of living according to her own wishes cannot be believed. Perhaps she has made up this story to show that she is a very simple and innocent woman. But if that is not so, then she is very cunning and dangerous. Now, this cannot be left as a doubtful case, and she cannot be allowed to go to her relatives.

"This woman has shown lot of concern and respect for you, and she has repeatedly begged you to meet her. She even said that she would do anything for you. It could be that she is genuine. Or maybe she wants to rope you in.

Both the possibilities have been considered at a very high level, and the decision has been taken to seek your help."

"What sort of help?" I asked.

"That you handle this case," my CO said.

"I am not trained for such a job," I told him.

"Yes, we know that, but you can be trained in a month or so. Look, Major Paawan, this is a rare opportunity for you to do something very important for the nation. Such opportunities do not knock at the door of everyone. You are very lucky. You have fought a war like a great hero and earned good name. I am sure that you would do equally well in this case also. Best of luck. You can now leave and start packing for your permanent posting."

"Sir, may I ask you a question?" I asked

"Yes, shoot."

"Is Rukhsana still in hospital?" I asked

"No, she has almost recovered, and she has been moved to Delhi."

"And where am I going?" I asked.

"Delhi, of course," my CO told me.

I went to my bunker. While packing, I started reflecting on the whole situation. I remembered when I had met her for the first time in the hospital. Several questions crossed my mind. I tried to find answers. I tried to construct an answer where I didn't find one. Naturally I took positive conclusions and imagined a good response for each question. I preferred the first assumption of my CO that she is genuine and innocent. I hoped her to be genuine and innocent.

Why should a highly educated, young and exceptionally beautiful girl like her indulge in ISI activities and put herself in a dangerous situation? She was indeed very beautiful, and highly intelligent, too. She could otherwise enjoy a really happy and peaceful life.

I had not found any other woman more charming than her. Her expressive and innocent looking blue eyes had special appeal. They were deeper than the deepest lake. Her long and thick black hair were like clouds that cover the vastness of the limitless sky. Her youthful body could be the envy of any beauty contestant anywhere. Her face was shining better than the full moon.

Why then did she take such a risky step? She would be foolish to do that. And I knew one thing - that she was not a foolish woman. Her mental abilities were much greater than those of an average human being.

She could weigh the options that were before her and - with the physical and mental assets that she had - she definitely had the best of all options before her. She could choose her life and could get married to the most eligible bachelor in her country, and enjoy the luxuries that life could provide. With such thoughts prevailing in my mind, I considered myself unsuitable for the job. But who would listen to me? I took a positive view and decided that I would start my job on the presumption that she was innocent; and if she turned out to be guilty, it would be her bad luck - because my country always came first and above all.

I reached Delhi at about 7:00 p.m. and was told that a very senior officer of the intelligence wing was waiting for me in a hotel.

On meeting me, he said, "I am very glad to meet you. From now on, you will report directly to me. There will be nobody in between. We will not meet in any office. You can call me on my particular phone number, which is for your calls only. Just say the relevant code word for meeting under normal conditions or for any emergency. Do not say anything on phone about our mission. Our mission is 'TOP SECRET.'

Take me as your uncle Ram Nath Mangal. Your father is my elder brother. Never call me 'sir.' Whenever we meet it will be a purely social meeting.

My wife and child will also behave with you in a similar manner. You will have dinner with us tonight, meet everybody, and be a member of my family. After that you will move to single officer's accommodation in the officers' mess, because you want to live independently. Any doubts so far?"

"None," I said.

"Good, your training will commence from the day after tomorrow. Not tomorrow, because there are some people coming to see you in my house.

"Remember, we are on a mission of national importance. Our relationship lasts till we breathe last," he said

"Yes, uncle. Can we go home now, I am starving," I said

"Yes, my son. Let us take off," he said.

When we reached home, I touched the feet of his wife, who hugged me with motherly affection and said, "she is Munny, your little sister. She studies in the tenth class."

Munny met me as if we were real cousins. She said that she was very happy to have a big brother. She showed me my room and told me to call her if I needed anything, as her room was next to mine. They did not have any servant for security reasons.

It is my habit to say my prayers every night before I go to sleep. After I had prayed I began to think about the family. I wondered why this senior vigilance officer had put everything on stake, including his entire family, for the sake of his country. His wife and young daughter fully support him and actively participate in his pursuit of excellence in his profession, at the risk of their own lives.

Lives of such officers are always gravely at risk, because it is not always possible to keep their operations hidden from enemy vigilance. They became my inspiration.

I looked up at the sky and wanted to talk to God. What does He want from me? Within a few days I had met two lots of people, who were well-educated, well-to-do and who could live happily and peacefully in society. They have many options available to them. But they have chosen to live the difficult way. I bowed my head before my Lord.

I was reminded of Gandhiji, the father of the nation. He, too, was highly educated and belonged to a well-to-do family, and could easily earn his living and enjoy his life with his dear ones. But why did he choose the most troublesome way for himself and his family? Many a time he was kicked and beaten. Most of the time, he and his wife spent in rotten jails. He too had put at stake everything that he had. Why? What for?

I was greatly impressed by all of them and at last I decided to plunge into the adventure fully and completely.

"Oh God, what do you want from me? I am ready to follow your ways," I said almost loudly.

"What happened brother?" Munny came running to my room.

"Nothing, my dear sister. I was just saying my prayers," I replied.

"You say your prayers so loudly? I thought you were shouting, or rather, crying," said Munny.

"Yes, my dear little sister, there are times in one's life when one wants to talk to God, one to one, and loudly enough, so that one can listen to Him, through oneself."

I noticed that my uncle and aunty were also standing near to us.

"Yes, son, you are absolutely right. So, what have you decided?" asked the aunty.

"I will do it. I am ready to do it, my uncle, sir," I said.

My aunty took Munny to her room, and both came back after some time. "Give this Geeta to your brother."

Munny came to me, hugged me, patted me on my cheek, and handed me the holy book, Geeta, saying, "Geeta will make my strong *bhaiya* much stronger. I think you need some rest." And they all left.

When I woke up the next day, Munny was about to give me a cup of tea. She kissed me on my cheek and asked, "did you have any sleep, or were you talking to your God?"

"Oh, I slept like a log of wood. Now there are no doubts, no confusions. Everything is very clear. I feel that I was born to do what I am doing now. The power of realisation makes you very strong. It seems as though you people were always with me," I said.

Munny said, "brother, how can it be that you meet someone for the first time and feel that he was always known to you? You came close so soon. It is very strange."

"Yes, Munny, these are the strange ways of God. Sometimes there are no logical explanations. But His ways are unique. He will put you on the track of the destination to which he wants to take you. It is best to go the natural way, as life comes. Anyway, where is the uncle?"

"He has gone to the railway station to meet some people. There is a pleasant surprise for you. Oh, I was not supposed to tell you. I am a fool. Mummy says that I can't digest any secret."

"Munny, you have told me half the secret; please tell me the remaining half also," I asked

And, hearing a knock on the door just then, she ran away to open it. I followed her and was really surprised when my parents walked in.

I touched the feet of my mother and father; and the exchange of glances was explanation enough: it told us all what the purpose of meeting was and what had been planned for the future.

I was meeting my parents for the first time after the war. My mother hugged me and said, "you always wanted a younger sister, and now you have one in Munny. She is very pretty."

"I wanted a little sister to fight with and beat, not one who will be my responsibility." Munny came and sat with me, and held my hand.

My parents lived there with me for one week, and then they left for our hometown, Dehradun. I moved to the officers' mess to live. I had a very busy schedule of training.

I was to use my emotional approach to discover her secrets, if there were any, which was a likelihood. Keeping in view national interests, I was prepared to use emotional blackmail, if necessary.

We had two objectives:

1. Firstly, to obtain as much information as possible about her and the enemy.
2. Secondly, to use her as our own agent, if possible.

It was a challenge to test my ability to achieve the objectives. Most of my training revolved around human behavioural techniques. My instructors felt that I was innately gifted with some of them.

I was given another letter from Rukhsana and with the instruction to reply to her this time. I should show that I had developed some interest in her.

In her second letter she had written, "my *masiha* (saviour), I begged you to meet me during our formal meeting last time, but you refused. Perhaps you were right. Why should you meet someone whom you do not even know, especially as I happened to be from your enemy country? You are perfectly right. But please understand the plight that I am going through. I wish, I seriously hope, that you would have left me to die. I do not know what to write and how to convince you to please meet me once, only once - please.

"Because somehow I feel that you can understand me. I told them everything correctly, but they do not believe a word from me. Why can't they verify the facts? Is it that the Indian army does not have any means to check? They can check my details and release me. I don't know how to put it to you? With what face should I write to you for help? I am giving this letter to the authorities to deliver to you, if they agree to do so. I am not even sure that the letter will reach you. If this letter reaches you and if you can consider it on humanitarian grounds, kindly meet me. Maybe, if you think that it would cause you embarrassment, please do not bother yourself, and consider that you have not received my letter.

"*Khuda hafiz* (God be with you),
Rukhsana."

I made a reply: "Rukhsana Begam, I received your two letters. I did not reply to your first letter because I didn't want to have anything to do with you. I must confess that you have a way with words; you have convinced me to meet you at least once, after I have obtained permission from my authorities. I hope that you will understand this necessity. I do not know whether I can be of any help to you. But maybe I should meet you once, as you have requested. I confess that you have awakened some interest in me to see you soon. I have applied for leave, and I will try to come sometime during the leave period.

"Best of luck,
Major Paawan."

I got a prompt reply, on the next day, "My dear lord - I think that I should call you that. You have been a brave soldier, and now I must say that you have proved yourself to be a man with guts and may be much more.

"I am anxiously waiting to meet you.

"*Khuda ka shukar hai jo unka paigam ayaa,*
"Marne wale ko jeene ka vadda ho jaise"

(Thank God that I received a message from you. It is like a new lease of life to the one who was about to die.) Thanks a million.

"Yours forever,
Rukhsana."

It was sometime in the evening that I was scheduled to meet her. No other officer was with me. She had been told in the morning that I was to come to meet her. When I had seen the last time, she was in white hospital sheets, and that evening she had put on a deep green Punjabi suit. She had let her hair loose and looked very attractive.

She received me with a long hug, "thanks, *moula* (God), at last He has sent you my way."

I asked, "why this closeness? Have we developed a relationship?"

"Maybe, fifty per cent from my side share," she said.

"I don't know what you mean. When we met the last time, you have shown overflowing gratitude. And today you talk like this? I don't understand you," I said.

"Keep meeting me, and you will begin to understand me better. The ways of nature are very strange. Everything is possible on this earth. Take me, for example; I never imagined that I would meet a man called Paawan, from a different country, on this earth, and that I would fall for him. Eh, tell me what does this word 'Paawan' mean?" she asked.

"It means pure," I told her.

"That is highly appropriate. I am sure that your parents have given you the most suitable name," she said.

"Apart from praising my name, why did you want to meet me?" I asked.

"I want to talk to you and tell you everything about me - my whole story. But first things first. Let me tell you something about myself. You see, I am a poet. Many of my poems have been published. Here are two lines for you. They are in Urdu. If you don't understand, ask me I will tell you the meaning. Don't hesitate! One cannot know all the languages of the world. I wrote it in the hospital after meeting you for the first time. I recite,

"*Khush nasib hum hain, jo aap se baat hui,*
Baad muddat, ik insaan se mulakat hui"

"It means that I consider myself lucky to meet you, because in you I have met a really good human being, after ages."

I asked her, "How do you know that I am a good human being? We have hardly met. You know nothing about me. Is it not pure flattery, as we say? But anyway, as far as the poetry goes, it is really a very good couplet."

She said, "you see, it was no flattery at all. A poet writes whatever impression he or she gets from what he or she observes. These are true inner feelings. I was sharing my first impression of you. You see, poetry is the most beautiful form of expression, and it is absolutely pure; rather, Paawan, it is the true impression of nature on the mind of the author. You will begin to understand poetry more if you keep meeting me. I will teach you to write poetry. I will instil poetry in you. It is such a wonderful and beautiful thing that you will start loving it."

"And to confess, I am already in love with poetry. I have been composing poetry since my childhood," I told her.

"Say something, please recite something. Anything, please, Paawan," she pleaded.

I said, "okay, for your flowing hair I would try to compose one. Please don't try to find mistakes, it may have weight problem, *huun* ... yes,

"*Ghataon se ghanne, shub se sia baal tere,*
Kehkshan jaise, lalchai hue arman mere."

(It means that your hair is thick like the clouds and black like the night. My emotions are swelling like the curves of the rainbow.)

"Oh, Allah; you are a genius, Paawan. Please forgive me for bragging about my poetry. I now know that I am nowhere near you. I didn't know you are such a master, a real *ustad*. Oh, *moula*, maybe this is why He forced me to take the step which I took. Maybe God Almighty himself guided me through this dangerous way to unite me with you. I understand now. *Toba, mere khuda; Toba Meri* (oh God, please pardon me). My belief in my *khuda* has become stronger now, after meeting you. I did not know that you knew Urdu so well. "Do they teach you Urdu here?" she asked.

"Yes, in almost all the states. There are many Urdu poets and authors of international fame in India. Tell me why did you want to meet me?" I asked.

"It was my inner instinct that I must meet you. But now, I think, I will always crave to meet you and try to be with you. You have brought so much pleasure, peace and solace to my life. You have invoked new faith and new interest in me. You have given new life to me. I think I am falling in love with you." She closed her eyes and tried to fall into my arms.

I pushed her away gently and said, "Isn't it becoming too much? I cannot imagine that a girl in captivity of an enemy country, and who is in interrogation custody, would let it be known that she has fallen in love with her interrogator. Do you think I would ever believe this?"

"Maybe not now, but it is true that I will one day prove it to you. You would have to believe me. And tell me, how are you, my interrogator? You came to meet me at my request. But please tell me, are you also one of them?" Suddenly she sounded suspicious.

"That is beside the point. You are a highly educated and bold lady. You cannot understand that I will not buy your story?" I asked her.

"Oh, for God's sake, please believe me, Paawan. I am seriously in love with you. You are the first and the last man in my life. I am sure that God made me to take such a risk just for you. Please, please believe me," she begged.

"You said you can prove it. How can you prove it, madam?" I asked.

"I told you that I can do anything for you. Anything means anything. What proof do you want from me? Tell me, what will satisfy you?" she asked.

"Rukhsana, can you … "

"Thank God, you called me by my name, for the first time. Thank you, Paawan. I love you. Before you put me to any test, please promise me one thing - that you will truly believe me," she said.

"Rukhsana, that depends on the degree of proof that you provide. If you convince me beyond an iota of doubt, I will certainly believe you," I told her.

"Okay, Paawan, come and sit near me. Please let me hold your hand so that, before you tell me to achieve the impossible, I have enough strength to do that. What is your wish my Lord?" she asked me.

"The first thing which you have to tell me is your exact purpose of crossing the border. Remember that what you have already told me in the past is not satisfactory. Do not repeat that story; it will not convince me. Tell me the truth, a convincing truth, and nothing else" I asked her.

"Oh *moula*, I don't know what you want from me. I give up to you as you wish, my Allah. Anyway listen to me, Paawan. You have really broken me. I will tell you everything truthfully and with perfect proof. Listen to me carefully, Paawan. I came to your country for the purpose of spying. I am an ISI agent."

She started talking. "I have been trained in this profession, and I was told to cross the border in such a way that your army authorities would believe that I had tried to cross the border for defection. I was to make you people believe that I was shot at by the Pakistani army while I was crossing the border. But no, they did not shoot me. I was meant to be injured, not killed. So, I shot myself with a pistol. That pistol must still be lying at the site where you found me injured. That .47 bore pistol will prove my story to you and convince you of my true love for you. My fingerprints will prove my statement beyond an iota of doubt. Paawan, please go and tell them to find that pistol, the proof of my love. Please, Paawan, please go now. I have not cried for many days; please leave me alone, my love."

I held her tight for a moment and left.

Flash messages were sent to the forward unit authorities. The pistol was found at the site and dispatched to our headquarters. The fingerprints on the pistol matched those of Rukhsana. The bullet which was extracted from the thigh of Rukhsana was fired from that pistol. There was no doubt left.

I went to see her again. She met me with great enthusiasm. I told her that the pistol had been found. The proof which she had provided was correct and convincing. I told her that I believed her completely.

Later, I gave her the good news that the authorities had allowed me to take her for an outing. She was very happy. I asked her where she wanted to go. But she said that she did not want to go to her relatives. She asked me to take her where ever I wanted. She expressed the feeling that her journey has ended. She has attained contentment. She told me that she is no longer bound by anyone now. She has now liberated herself. She was now totally independent from previous relationships and duties and would henceforth live as I wanted her to live.

I hardly believed in my good luck that I was successful so soon. I tried to take her into my arms and asked her, "What do you think that the enemy agents be thinking about you?"

"I think they have already caught my trail, and it is owing to your tight protection that I am still alive," she said.

"With that point in mind, would you like to go out into the open?" I asked her.

"Yes, why not? Paawan, dear, the safest place to hide is in the open, among the public, where you are least expected. Please don't take me to a place which you have already planned," she suggested.

"I think you are right, dear?" I said.

"What a darling you are! This is the first time that you have called me dear. I really love you, love you very much, more than my own self. God has been so good, so kind in giving you to me."

"You are a strange woman. You can think of romance even when your life is under threat," I said.

"Oh, sweetheart, death is going to come anyway, anytime, unexpectedly. So why should you trouble your mind about it? Make the best use of the present. What about taking me out darling? In which vehicle are we travelling?" she asked.

"Initially it is an army load carrying truck, and after making sure that we are not being followed, we will change over to a civil car. That car will at first travel ahead of our vehicle, and after about five kilometres, we will stop for the changeover," I told her.

When I took over the wheel of the car, I changed over to my second choice of destination. We were booked into a government guest house there. From there, I was free to proceed to any place, as long as I kept in touch with uncle. I was to contact him at least once in a day, and report to him the details of whatever I found out from her. She was very happy to be out under the open sky, among the hills with thick forests and a very fresh cool air, full of fragrance.

She said, "your India is beautiful. This place is heaven."

"Don't you want to know the name of the place?" I asked.

"No, beauty has only one name. That is beauty. I have always dreamt of a place like this." She started singing a sweet melody. It was a full moon night in the month of May. We walked through the jungle for quite some time and returned to our room late at night. When we woke up the next day it was almost lunchtime.

"Do you think they will have a good beauty parlour here?" she asked.

"No, I don't think so; it is a small place. But why do you want to spoil your natural beauty. You look gorgeous, anyway." I said.

"Thanks, darling, it is a great compliment from the man whom I love. You called me beautiful for the first time. I love you. You see, I feel that I must change my appearance and roam about freely. They must have started their second plan by now," she told me.

"And what was their first plan, darling?" I asked.

"Oh ... I will die for that word. Call me 'darling' again and take out from me whatever you want. I am all yours," she said.

"Darling, sweetie; you just mentioned about the plans. Their first plan and second plan ... ?" I asked.

"Why are you in such a hurry? Why don't you enjoy fully what nature is offering you, lucky man? The more information you take from me, the more you are pushing me towards my end. You see, the things have happened so unbelievably fast that I can hardly believe that it is not a dream, but is actually happening to me in my real life. I came for a different purpose, and I can see where I have ended up now. These are the strange ways of the Almighty. I don't know how long it is going to last. Paawan, I have a very sincere request and I beg you to grant me my wish, please," she begged.

"Yes, darling; tell me, what do you want?" I asked.

"Please promise me that you will never leave me. On my part I will do whatever you say. Your smallest wish will be a command for me. It is a fact that I cannot live without you. It seems to me like a nightmare. Paawan; let us make the best of these beautiful moments which God has granted to us. It looks as if it will end as suddenly as it has happened," she said.

"How ridiculous. Why do you talk like this? Do you think that you are not safe with me? Do you think I can't save you?" I got annoyed.

"Yes, my love. That is just what I think. You see, when I left my home and my people, I told them that we were meeting for the last time, because the path which I had chosen always ended like that," she said.

"No I will not let that happen. Don't worry. And tell me what their plans were," I said.

She said, "You are so professional. Okay, my love, if that is your wish. I take it as your command to me. The first plan was that, after entering India the way I did, I would apply for asylum, and once I had achieved that, I would marry someone from the defence forces with the help of my relatives here. My real strategy would be implemented only then. I was to gather information pertaining to planning and deployment of troops and pass it on to the agents.

"Here I want to rectify a lie which I have I told you at the initial stages. You see, my father is very much alive and he is a brigadier in that army. He forced me to do all this. It was a sort of indoctrination. I was given rigorous training, and rated among the world-class espionage operators. This is my second visit to your country. On the previous occasion I had come on a valid passport and visa. I have stayed here for three months. One month on my visa and two months on an extension for medical reasons. I was told that I had done a wonderful job for them. They selected me this second time and told me that it was the last time. They inducted me for good, so that, I could become permanent source of information for them. The second time ... I think I am tired. I am falling asleep; take me in your arms. Perhaps I am dying." She fell asleep suddenly, as if she was drugged.

I tried to make her comfortable in my arms and played with her hair with gentle touch so as not to disturb her. In her sleep, she looked like a beautiful fairy from heavens. It was a too enchanting experience for me. In my heart, I wished that she was not from the enemy country. I wished that she was out of our own clan, and one of us - the one whom society would accept and the one whom I could have.

Leaving her fast asleep, I went out to call my uncle. Unfortunately he was not available on the telephone number which he had given me. I called his home. Aunty picked up the phone. She was crying bitterly. I asked her what the matter was. She told me that Munny was missing from the home since yesterday. I told her that I am on my way back, but she informed me that the uncle had gone to trace her and had given strict instructions that I should stay wherever I was and not worry about anything.

I knew that something like that would happen to them, but I had hoped that it would not happen that soon. I was burning with anger. I did not understand why uncle had made his family members a party to the dangerous job that he was doing. Was that a part of his official duties?

After coming back to the room, I found that Rukhsana was sleeping calmly, with her long hair spread all over the bed, and both her arms stretched out along her tall body. In the yellow light, she was looking like a witch who had her tummy full of blood and flesh. How I hated her! Thinking what drama she had played with me recently of showing her sincere love. I loved to hate her. I shouted at the top of my voice to wake her up.

"What happened darling? You are looking very upset. What happened?" she asked.

"It is all because of you." I sounded very angry.

"What is because of me, darling? What have I done, my love?" she asked.

I told her that my sister has been kidnapped, and that I blamed her for that. She is the one who had started all that. She made me narrate to her what aunty had told me.

"Calm down, my sweet heart. Your sister is safe. Don't you understand what your uncle has told you? That you should not worry at all and keep staying wherever you are. That means that he knows where she is. And tell me, my love, who is this uncle of yours who instructs you like a boss? He seems to be from the forces. Is he from my profession?" she asked.

"What rubbish you talk. You always keep imagining, everybody like you. There are people who have many other professions than spying," I said.

"Okay, don't tell me. Please go again and try to speak to your uncle," she told me.

I went out and rang up my uncle. Luckily he was available and assured me that Munny was perfectly alright; and he told me not to call him abruptly. I was also told to move out from that place and call him again the next day at a particular time.

When I had told Rukhsana all that, she was simply happy and told me that one must not distrust the one whom he loves.

On the next day I drove her to another far-flung place - a famous hill station. Her attitude, her intimate behaviour, and her total surrender were affecting me like a magic force. She would insist that I take her for a walk through the jungle, in a full moon night; and there she recited to me the sweetest songs. She told me that she had composed those songs for me.

The nights were not very chilly, but cold enough to make you seek the physical warmth of your companion. I was certain that life could not be more pleasant and more romantic than that. Was this the ultimate heaven? Can a human being desire more than this from life? I did not realise when I fell in love with her.

We stayed there for three days. I started developing more faith in her, as she looked open and prepared to tell me all that she knew.

She said that she wanted to meet my parents. I spoke to my uncle who agreed and told me that he would also come and meet us there.

I drove her to Dehradun. On reaching the city, she told me that she wanted to visit IMA, where her father had been trained as an officer. I made clear to her that was not possible. She accepted without argument. She met my parents with great respect and hugged my mother, and started crying bitterly. My mother tried to comfort her, but her sobs were not coming to an end. My mother took her to her room to rest, but she could not hold her tears. After some time she slept there as if she was too tired and longing to have such rest. She looked very calm in her deep sleep.

I told my parents that what started from the hostilities of war, and from job requirements, has ended as a love affair.

My father advised me that the realities should not be forgotten. One life is not sufficient to achieve everything that you want to achieve. Maybe, many lives could also not achieve anything. Some beautiful scenes of nature were often short-lived. It is wise not to take hasty decisions. We must learn to control our emotions. Never run after mirages - they are not real.

I understood what he meant, but was not quite able to put his advice into practice.

After two days, Uncle Mangal came. He told us that Munny had not been kidnapped but had been moved to the place where Rukhsana had been kept before. That had been done to deceive anyone who might have been on the watch.

I fought with him and made him promise not to repeat such incidents, involving Munny or aunty.

It was afternoon teatime when my father introduced Uncle Mangal to Rukhsana: "He is my younger brother and has come here for a few days in connection with his business."

She got up and went to him to shake hands. "In what business are you, uncle? I was told that your daughter had gone missing. How is she now?"

"I am an author. I write stories. Munny is fine. Paawan must have told you that," he said.

"Uncle, please do not include real characters in your stories. It hurts so terribly sometimes. They become your weakness at times and totally change what you originally wanted to write. Paawan was so furious that he would have killed me for something that I didn't do," she said.

Uncle Mangal said, "Rukhsana, you have been very cooperative. Thanks for that. I do not know whether it is because of Paawan, or for some other reason, or may be it is your third plan. Incidentally you have not told him about your second plan. Be a nice girl, and please tell us,"

"Oh uncle, you are also like him. He is always in a great hurry. You have met me only five minutes ago and now you want to finish off in a moment. Please let me live for some more time. I know, I am like a forth degree cancer patient for whom there is no cure. I will definitely not live for long. Don't you think I deserve more time, after I have behaved as I did."

"Yes, I understand. I agree with you completely. Take your time. And in the meantime, if you will permit us, I have to go to the market to buy a pineapple cake for Paawan - Munny has instructed me to buy one for her brother. Paawan can you please accompany me? I do not know the shop," he said.

He told my mother: "Please take good care of Rukhsana, as she is the most special guest for us." When we came out of the house, I noticed two or three unknown faces around the house. Uncle told me not to worry about them, because they were his men.

On the way to the market he explained, "You see, she is the most precious catch for us, and we cannot take any chances. You have handled her very well. She would have never broken under any pressure or strictness. Your charm and emotional treatment have worked. Keep the pressure on and get as much information as you can. You should now try to find out about her second plan - what she hinted at the last time. I will hang around outside so that you can have free time with her.

When I was alone with her, I asked her to tell me about her little sister. Does she look like her and how old is she?

"Oh, she is my little doll. She is my pet, like a small parrot. She repeats what I say, she sings what I sing. She resembles me so much that she is almost my duplicate. She will be turning twenty next month. I do not know where I will be at that time. Paawan, all these years I have been doing everything for her. Mummy did not spare any time for us from her kitty parties and other social work. You see, I used to give her a bath when she was small, dress her and prepare her lunch for school. She too has very long and thick hair, like mine. I used to do her hair, tie her plat, and play with her hair.

"My father has been most unreasonable with both of us. He forced me into this shit. I don't want my sister to be put into this dangerous job. Paawan, I love her. I want to meet her. I want to warn my father to keep away from her. I want to tell my Ameena to save herself from him. Paawan, please I want to go back to her."

She started crying like a homesick mother who had been separated from her kids. I removed her tears, I tried to make her conformable; and after some time her sobs could not prevent her from falling into a deep sleep in my lap.

On the next day, she was working in the kitchen with my mother. She insisted on cooking all the meals. At dinner, she prepared the favourite dishes for the uncle. He was surprised and asked Rukhsana whether there was any special reason for that.

"Yes uncle, I want a special favour from you. You have to give me an honest promise," she said.

"Yes Rukhsana, tell me what do you want?"

"Is that a God promise?"

"Yes, it is my God promise to you. I will grant you one wish if it is in my power," said Uncle Mangal.

"Uncle, please don't drag your daughter into this. Please do not put my Paawan's Munny into such dangerous situations. She reminds me of my own little sister Ameena." And she started crying and could not control her sobs. It was very difficult to control her hysteria. My mother took her to her bedroom. She put her into her lap, and after some time she was fast asleep. She slept with my mother that night.

The next day at the breakfast table, my uncle repeated his promise. She went to him and gave him a tight hug of thanks.

Uncle said, "I feel a girl like you deserved much better from life."

"I cannot ask God for anything else, after meeting Paawan. May be, He had planned my destiny this way. Uncle, after breakfast we can do some talking, if you want."

"Yes, yes. Let us sit in the study; come, Paawan," said my uncle.

After the three of us had sat down conformably in the study room, Rukhsana started narrating, "I had mentioned to Paawan that I had second plan. The second possibility for me was that I would not be taken as a defector and would be arrested. That would be the outcome if I do not succeed in convincing the authorities to give me asylum. My job was not to give out anything under any circumstances. But if, by any chance, the Indian authorities were able to find out my exact status, and if I was arrested, a rescue operation would start for me. I would try my best to escape, or they would try to secure my release. I am sure that they have realised that I am in captivity. There is a possibility that they are searching for me. I really do not know what they would be planning."

"You are right: we have caught an agent soon after you people had left. He confessed that they had the instructions to kill you at first sight."

"I knew my father would do that," she said.

"What is your father?" uncle asked her.

"He is the number two in ISI," she said.

Uncle Ram Nath said, "Okay, Rukhsana, just listen to me carefully. You see, you are in such an invidious situation that, if we put you on a trial, you would be either hanged, or at least imprisoned for life. And if your people find you, they would undoubtedly try to kill you. One way or the other, we come to the same point. What do you want to do now?"

She said, "you are right, uncle. But is there no way out? Incidentally, please forgive me for asking. What is your position in the department?"

"It is the same as that of your father; hence you can depend on me, and you may know that, whatever I say, I have the authority to say it. You asked me for the way out. I can suggest to you one way out. But before I make that suggestion, I want one absolutely honest reply from you," he said.

Rukhsana said, "anything uncle, sir. I promise on my almighty God that I will speak the truth."

"Tell me how much do you love Paawan, and what can you do for him?" he asked.

"Sir, I love him more than my own life, and I can do anything for him. I am sure about that. I can give my life for his sake, anytime, any day, provided that makes him happy," she said.

"Then listen to me carefully. To satisfy the law of the land and to prove that you are useful to this society and have a right to breathe freely in this country, you have to do similar operations for this nation with full sincerity," Uncle Mangal said.

"I think you are right. That is the only way out for me. What do you say, Paawan?" she asked.

I said, "I am sure that both of you are right. I would hate to put you in any more danger; but it seems that we do not have any other choice."

"Okay then, I will leave for my headquarters today and plan out details for you." He said and left.

We stayed in our house for a week or so and then moved to another secret destination. She told me many more useful matters, which I passed on to my uncle. By then he, too, had begun to trust her completely. After a few days uncle met us again. He explained that the plan was ready and that they were now working out the details for the execution of the plan. He gave us the outlines. Rukhsana would escape from our custody in a most natural way. She would then try to implement the second plan. She would go to her closest relatives and live with them and re-establish contact with enemy agents.

In the meantime, she would pass on to us whatever instructions she gets. We would try to place Paawan at a location from where it would be easier for him to develop contacts with Rukhsana. She would try to convey to her father's agents that she is in a position to establish links in the defence forces. The detailed instructions would follow later when the right time came. After that, a month passed.

One day I told her that I would not be meeting her quite so often any more and that I would soon move to my new place, on transfer.

She looked very sad. Suddenly her eyes were full of tears. "Is that the beginning of our permanent separation, my love?"

"No, it may rather be the beginning of our permanent union. Now the test for you begins; you must prove that you are working honestly for this country and that the law of the land should adopt you." I said.

"Are you with me?" she asked me.

"Yes, of course I am with you. The execution of the plan has begun. I will be placed beforehand at the place where you have chosen to stay after your escape - your grandmother's city, Lucknow. There, we will meet in a natural way. I will create such a situation that I can meet your grandmother or your maternal uncle before your planned escape. I will establish contacts with them and arrange a situation in which they will introduce you to me. Then we start meeting with the acceptance of your family. Uncle's contacts would keep briefing you from time to time." I gave her a long hug and we departed.

I was posted at Lucknow in a department where some contacts with the general public were possible. I stayed in the officers' mess and became the regular visitor of the local club.

One of the Sundays, when I was returning from the club, a car hit my motorbike from behind. I fell down and my left arm got fractured. The way in which it happened was that a truck tried to overtake the car, and while trying to save himself, the car driver banged into me.

An old lady and a man in his mid-forties came out of the car, and they took me to a nursing home for treatment. They looked after me and were highly apologetic. The old lady insisted on taking me to her *havelli* (a large house). There I was introduced to other family members, but I could not find the one that I was looking for. The old lady was very affectionate and insisted that I call her grandmother and should visit them very often.

I said, "'grandmother' is too long a name and that I would like to call her Granny, and that, because that sounded like oldies, I would just call her Ni." Everybody laughed.

Soon I became an almost regular visitor to their house. All my Sundays were spent with them. Whenever there was a Sunday on which I missed going to them, they would complain about my not going there. And whenever they had a picnic or any other outings, they always insisted to take me along.

On instructions from uncle, I told them that I was going on some training to Bangalore for two months and would hence miss them. I first went to Bangalore and then returned to Dehradun, to my parents, for a two-months holiday. I knew that this was done for the settlement of Rukhsana in that family.

When I returned, I rang the grandmother and informed her that I had come back. She hesitated for a while and then told me to visit them next Sunday, because they were going out that day. In the following week I again I rang up, and that time granny called me for dinner. At the dining table the grandmother introduced me to her.

"Meet my sister's granddaughter, Roshanara. My sister stays in Muradabad. She has come here for her higher studies and will stay with us."

"*Adaab*," she said.

"*Tasleem*," I replied

I noticed that she had changed her appearance. She had gotten her long hair cut to a boy's hairstyle. She was wearing jeans and a short T-shirt. She looked pretty in that outfit. I tried to control my heartbeat – my heart was thumping like the air pump of an ironsmith.

"You are looking very pretty. People in Muradabad are more modern than in Lucknow, isn't it, Ni? I think we live in the sixteenth century, and we are quite backward," I said.

Uncle Aslam (grandmother's son) replied, "yes, you are right, and more poetic also. You see, our Roshanara is very good poetess, like you. I am sure that you two will enjoy each other's company."

All the youngsters started insisting that both of us recite something. Uncle also supported them.

Roshanara recited,
"Kash aa jai yakeen, unko meri wafai ka.
Bin dekhe kar lete hain, yakeen jaise khudai ka."

(I wish he may believe in my faithfulness, just as we all believe in the existence of God without seeing). All appreciated and clapped. They started looking at me for a suitable reply.

I said, *"Tum par yakeen hai, jaise khud par yakeen hai, Main jo kuchh bhi hun, bus tu bhi wahi hai."*

(I believe in you as I believe in myself. Whatever I am, you are the same.) Grandma got up and blessed both of us. She declared that some day, they would organise a poetry competition for both of us and call other relatives also, and arrange a grand function.

This was perhaps the beginning of our second phase of happiness. Or maybe it was the start of uncle's real operations. We started to meeting again frequently, sometimes in the presence of the family members and sometimes without telling them.

She had written so much romantic poetry for me. She used to sing to me in the sweetest melody. Whenever we met, it felt as if it was the first meeting, and each meeting was more interesting than the previous one. When we departed we looked forward to the next meeting with eager anticipation. She was now more willing to cooperate. Uncle Mangal met both of us whenever he wanted to meet and discuss further plans.

At first, her father was happy, but after some time he started pressurising her for important information. She told me her fear that her father might have started having doubts about her.

The order was conveyed to her that the third phase of the plan must commence. That meant getting married to a defence officer and creating a long-term information source.

I discussed the matter with uncle. He was against the marriage aspect of the plan, because his intention had been to send her back to Pakistan and to obtain the latest information on policy matters pertaining to defence in this way.

This became a very crucial issue. Two giants were getting restless to strike at each other. I asked uncle to tell us what the best course of action would be for us.

He suggested that she should convey to them that consent for marriage has been received, but that, before getting married, she wanted to visit that country and meet her mother and sister. She conveyed this intention to the agents, and after a few weeks she received a positive response.

The documents for her visit were issued in the name of Roshanara.

The next time when I met uncle I got a feeling that he was not completely ready to depend upon her. I suggested that he could have another meeting with her to reassure himself. He agreed and the meeting was arranged.

The uncle asked her how she would react if her father accused her of passing the information on to us.

"I would simply deny it, and he would believe me because I have been successful in achieving the given task. His instructions were to escape if I am arrested, get lost in the public, take shelter in some relative's place, and develop connections with a serving officer of the defence forces. I think, I have done all that."

"But how can you make me believe that you will be sincere to us after reaching the other side?"

"That is a professional question. My dear uncle, sir; my work will speak. Don't you feel that whatever I have done so far is sufficient proof of my loyalty? And as far as the faith is concerned, Paawan will vouch for that."

"That is what I am coming to. I suggest that Paawan should also go with you," the uncle said.

She said, "that is the most dangerous thing to do. It will create doubts about my link with your department. By now, all of their agents must be having a photograph of Major Paawan in their pockets. They would only be too pleased to lay their hands on him and use third and fourth degree inhuman methods on him. They would try to take out everything from him in days what they expect me to achieve in a lifetime. And besides, Paawan, don't you have any other watchdogs already operating there? You should, if you don't have any. I am sure you are going to have me watched, anyway."

That sounded very logical. Uncle agreed to let her go. Loose ends were tied up. Uncle gave her a final briefing on how to obtain, safeguard and pass on the information, and what the code words were, etc.

I told Rukhsana that it was going to be very difficult for me to live without her, especially because I would be really worried about her safe return.

"My love, I think uncle made a big mistake in recruiting you. I will tell him to discharge you from this profession. Darling, in this line, preference is given to the safeguarding of information, rather than to the preservation of human life."

I said, "I can never understand you. Sometimes I feel that you love life so much, and other moments I feel that you do not care about life at all. I cannot imagine how you can use all the adjectives like 'darling, my love' etc. in such circumstances."

"Oh Paawan, you are so loving and innocent. I told you earlier that life is highly uncertain and that it can end suddenly any time; and hence it is highly unfaithful. So why care about it? It is the present moment - that is what life is. Tomorrow will never come, as it will always remain a day after today. You say I don't love life. Maybe you are right, because I live life rather than love it. Don't try to weaken me, Paawan. Say good-bye to me. Here are all the poems that I have written for you. Read them when I am away," she told me.

I had read many detective stories of world-class detectives, but I could never imagine how they lived life under the constant threat of death. I thought that this profession was for those daredevils who were prepared not to care for their lives as much as for information. Only then did they have the right to join this profession.

Finally, she had to leave. There was no news about her for about two months after she left. One day, suddenly, the uncle summoned me. He gave me a small slip that was written by Rukhsana. She had scribbled, "Paawan, I am scribbling this in a great hurry. I pray that it reaches you. My father has found out the facts and issued orders to kill me. God, save Ameena from him. Darling, I will meet you in the next life. Take care; don't cry for me, it would hurt my soul, my love. I will mingle with the air that you breathe. Yours Rukh...."

After that I did not hear anything about Rukhsana; I did not hear what exactly had happened to her. I thought that she might have been in custody at a secret place. The uncle was happy with her work. She had proved her loyalty.

Many times I asked the uncle about her, but he tried to avoid the topic. However, finally he gave way and said, "Major Paawan, you may blame me for sending her, but I never thought that she would break under the pressure. Her father forced her to prepare her younger sister for joining her profession. But she refused to do that. She also refused to continue with the work. I think her father has thought her to be dangerous because of the secrets which she knew, so he got her killed. Her mother and sister were told that she had gone to India."

Nearly six months passed. One evening, at about 7:00 p.m. I received a call from the grandmother. She was trembling while she spoke and she breathed heavily. "Listen to me carefully: She has returned. I have received a phone call from her. She wants to meet you immediately and has said that you should not inform anybody else. Go alone. She is waiting for you in the hotel 'City Town,' room number thirteen."

I thought for a moment of informing the uncle, but then I remembered her instructions. I was confused. Did uncle tell me a lie about her death? Maybe she is alive. She must have forbidden me to inform anybody. It must be for security reasons. I rushed to the hotel.

She opened the door when I knocked. The room was dimly lit. She asked me to close the door and sit on the sofa opposite where she was sitting.

I said, "Why this much distance? We are meeting after ages. In fact I had lost the hope of ever meeting you again. Uncle gave me bad news about you. How are you? Say something! Why are you keeping quiet?" I got up and tried to go near her.

"Stay where you are, Major Paawan." Her stern voice warned me. I felt as though heavens had fallen on me. This voice did not belong to Rukhsana.

"Who are you? Where is Rukhsana?" I asked.

"You are asking me, 'where is Rukhsana'? I have crossed the world and come to you to ask this question. Tell me where is my *appa* (sister), Major Paawan?"

"Are you Ameena?" She looked like Rukhsana. I tried to go to her.

"Stay put where you are. I have a loaded gun. You have recognised me correctly. I am Ameena. Now you tell me: Where is my Appa? She has told me many things about you. She sincerely did everything for you, whatever you people wanted her to do. You used her. She gave her love to you, and you betrayed her," she said.

I was surprised, "I betrayed her? How did I betray her? I too loved her truly."

Suddenly there was a knock at the door. She got up and showed me a pistol in her hand; it was aimed at me. She signalled to me with the pistol that I should hide behind the curtains and not utter a word. I obeyed.

A waiter entered the room and said, "Madam, further instructions have come; read them carefully and act accordingly. The next contact time is tomorrow at 6:00 p.m., in Rani Park." Then the waiter left.

It was not difficult for me to figure out that her father had brainwashed her and had inducted her to do spying for that country. She must have come for spying.

She said again, "come on, Major Paawan, you have to answer a few questions before I take my revenge from you for killing my Appa. Tell me how you killed her, so that I can devise similar death for you."

"No, I did not do anything to her. How could I kill someone whom I loved so much?" I said.

"Don't you have any morals? You got her killed and are now telling me that you loved her so much. She gave you her love, her faith, and she did exactly what you people wanted her to do."

I got angry and almost shouted at her, "Oh, you shut up ... what rubbish you are talking. Please, for God's sake, listen to me. It was not, me."

She said angrily, "you people called her here. She came for you. Only for you - and you got her killed here in your own country. I have come to your home to take my revenge. Now remember her, recollect how she would have felt before dying."

She shot at me, injuring me at the left shoulder. I fell down. "Oh, Ameena dear, my little doll; I didn't do anything to your Appa. It was your father. Your father got her killed. See - her letter written to me. Read this."

She read the letter and started crying like a small kid.

"Oh Paawan, please forgive me. I understand the reality now."

Without wasting any time she took me to the hospital. I gave a statement to the police that I had shot myself by accident.

I told everything in detail to uncle when he came to the hospital. Ameena also explained to us everything in detail. Her father had brainwashed her and had convinced that the Indians had killed her Appa. He prepared her for coming to India so that she could take revenge and use her for spying. She was told by the uncle to stay with her grandmother and maintain regular contact with me, in disguise, as Rukhsana had done in the past.

We had long discussions about all that had happened in the past. Uncle suggested that Ameena should now go back to that country and follow the footsteps of Rukhsana, and take real revenge from the actual killers of her sister.

Ameena said that she was ready to do anything. I protested. I told Ameena everything that Rukhsana had said about her. I told Ameena that Rukhsana never wanted her sister also to enter this dangerous profession.

Uncle argued that she has already entered the profession. Now there is no going back. If we let her off now, the enemy would not allow her to survive: she would meet the same fate as her sister. She knows many of their secrets. They would eliminate her. The best option for her was to continue to work for us as her sister did.

Ameena agreed to do what uncle told her to do. She was briefed to pass on all details about the activities of the agents who came in contact with her. All her activities were to be monitored through me, so I pretended before her grandmother family that I took her as Roshanara. I had maintained my normal behaviour with them.

We started to meet more often. Whenever we met, Rukhsana was always the main subject of our discussion. I started telling her in more detail about my past meetings with Rukhsana.

We went to the places which Rukhsana and I had visited earlier. We read each and every line of poetry that she had written and given to me. Ameena used to sing to me whenever I asked her. Her voice was husky rather than clear, and as thin as that of Rukhsana, but it had more depth and was very soothing.

I took her to the hill station where we had gone for the first time. We went to the jungle for a walk in the evening. I told her, "Rukhsana has called this spot a heaven, and today when she has gone to the real heaven, I feel that she is present somewhere around us."

I asked her to sing the following few lines of my poetry:
"Jaane is mahol mein, kiya khas baat hai,
Dil aaj aapke bin, bahut udaas hai,
Aa to rahi hai khushbu, hawa men tumhari,
Lagta hai jaise tu kahin aas paas hai"
(I do not know what is special in these surroundings. Today I am missing you the most. Your fragrance has spread in the air, as it seems that you are somewhere around us.)

Ameena sang those lines for me again and again. Every time she sang the lines in a different tune, giving them a classical touch, and making the poetry more enchanting, more soothing. Later, when we returned to the hotel room, she said to me, "Paawan, my Appa used to share everything with me. She gave me all that belonged to her. I almost got used to depending on her belongings, and I felt that everything that she had would ultimately come to me."

"What are you trying to say?" I asked.

"Exactly what you have understood," she said.

"But I am not a property. Love cannot be inherited. It cannot be shared, and it cannot be passed on," I said.

"Here you are wrong. The children inherit the love of their forefathers and parents. It is always shared by the living people. On the other hand, hatred is the child of anger; it is always temporary, always short-lived, as time is the killer of hatred. But love is nurtured by time. Paawan, to confess to you, let me tell you that when Appa was alive, and when she used to talk to me about you, I always had a sense of belonging in my mind, subconsciously, and a sense of some sort of right on you, or of an inexplicable attraction towards you. I believed that on some day or other, you would come to me forever. Unknowingly, you became a part of me long ago, before I had not even met you. Paawan, let us face the truth: don't you think that the soul of Appa would be pleased to see us united, rather than me married to a different person and you also tying the knots of marriage with some other woman?" she asked.

I found her arguments absolutely persuasive; hence I made no reply. She insisted, "why don't you say something? You army people do not take long to make a decision, I am sure. You must decide now because time never waits for anybody. It is the present that is life, because tomorrow will never come - it will always remain a day after today."

I felt that she was talking exactly like her sister. She looked like her sister's duplicate. But can the duplicate replace the original? The similarity influences the mutual sense of attraction. If two people have similar likes, similar habits, and know each other well, they are bound to be attracted. My mind kept arguing.

"What are you thinking, Paawan? Do you think what I said was wrong? Tell me honestly: Do you think you would ever be able to marry someone else? You know, Appa once wrote,

*"Kurbat se paida hui mohabbat, kurbat se phalli phuli,
jab se tum gai bidesh, hammari sudh budh bhuli,"*
(It is with closeness that love happens and develops. And since the time when you have gone away, you have forgotten me.)

She sang some other songs for me. She put her arms around me and took me in her lap. I felt a sort of deep touch - so sweet, so soothing, so piercing to the soul. And I felt that she was with me, in me, my own Rukhsana, my own Ameena, my own self.

I kept thinking, 'Is it love again? Has it happened again? Is it a mere attraction? Or is it real love? But what is the difference? The state of acute attraction is love. Love is attraction. Everything that is united is united due to the love. Physical bodies are not permanent; hence they must change their forms. Rukhsana has changed her form. Ameena has to change her form. I must change my form.

Then why should physical bodies exist? They exist because they have to achieve a purpose, as Rukhsana has once said. She has achieved a purpose and left. We are alive because we have not achieved that purpose completely. What is the purpose? It is Karma (duty). What is my Karma? To do my duty towards the nation to which I belong.

I suddenly felt that I must call the uncle immediately and ask him when Ameena will leave? Do I also have to go? The uncle was happy about our decision. He got busy in making the plans for the move.

The two giants were again ready to strike. Again, the stage was all set again. The directors fastened the chords to their fingers, ensuring that the other ends were tightly fixed to the puppets. The show must go on.

7

Double Standards

It is a strange world. Religious books, and the people to whom other people like to listen, and in whom they like to believe, say that God the Almighty created this world. Man the wisest of all creatures discovered and developed knowledge. Knowledge gave names and meanings to everything and defined all activities. Philosophers have preached certain acts as good while others as bad and immoral.

Another strange thing is that these definitions and beliefs keep changing with time and situation, and with the attitude of every human being. Similar things acquire different meanings for the same individuals in different situations. Sometimes, we modify our view for our convenience, and to suit ourselves.

Take me for example: I was a firm believer in the value of purity, social justice and truth. When I began to look for a marriage partner, my first priority was that she should be a virgin girl. When I was of marriageable age, my parents introduced many girls to me, but none satisfied my conditions. I wanted to tie the knot of marriage without compromising my principles. Time rolled on until, when my number came up, I was already thirty five years old.

I fell for the daughter of a newly-posted JCO (junior commissioned officer) in our unit. She was a beautiful, young and educated girl. Since ours was a combined family, and as we cared for each others' opinions, my marriage to her had the approval of other members of my family also.

Radhika came into my life like gradually spreading morning sunlight on my earth. I considered that it was worth waiting for her, because I had found my ideal match in her. I was a happy man, satisfied with myself and my family, except my sister, who was a widow of an army man.

My father advised us to look for a match for her re-marriage. We were all proud of my brother-in-law's gallantry, but now the most important issue was the life of a young woman.

Death is dead end in itself, but life is a new start at every moment.

My father initiated the dialogue, but there was resistance from my mother and from the elder sister of my father, who lived with us because she was a divorcee. I knew the reason for their opposition. Ours was a lower middle class family, and we did not have liberal means for our keep. Being an NCO (non-commissioned officer) in the army, my pay was not quite sufficient to support my entire extended family of ten persons.

The life pension of my sister was good money for meeting the expenses of our large family. All in our family were quite educated, and we understood that if my sister was to get married again, she, and hence our family, as a whole, would lose her pension. Some in our family openly objected to the idea of my sister's re-marriage, but several of us, including myself, did not have the courage to actually to state the reason for our objection. My father argued that my sister had a long life to live and that it is not right to force her to spend her youth without a male companion, but chose to remain a passive listener, thinking that it would be difficult to find someone who would accept my sister easily. The question of losing the pension also influenced our minds. The conflict carried on for a few years.

My wife, Radhika, argued in favour on my father's opinion and said that the girl too wanted to get married; therefore we should do something. I shouted at her for raising the issue once again and pointed out that it would be difficult to find someone who would accept a 'second-hand wife.'

This made Radhika agitated, and she asked me, "Are you the same man who talked about morality and social justice? And today you do not hesitate to call your sister 'second-hand'?

"So what is wrong? May be my words are not very decent but those convey the direct meaning. Take my personal example, I married you because you were virgin." I told her.

On this she further got furious and said, "How did you know that? The difference is that you did not know the facts at that time and now in this case it is an open secret."

I had the worst shock of my life.

She continued, "Many a time, I tried to tell you the truth-when you proposed to me, and even after our marriage, but at that time, your priorities were different. You were not prepared to invest your time to listen to me, because your physical desire was so strong. Perhaps you were madly in love with me and did not care about listening to anything. Certain things did not mean anything to you then.

"Now our ties are stronger because of our kids. Our love has grown exponentially. Please understand that I am speaking for the good of your own sister. Or maybe you can say that a woman is fighting the cause of a woman. Being a woman, I understand her position better than you.

"Please, for God's sake, do not shy away from doing your duties because of certain material considerations. A woman is unhappy because of a certain act of which you and the authorities think that it is a real favour to her. I want my man to stand up boldly for the same values that he used to defend earlier. I do not want my man to succumb to circumstances and to opportunely give different meanings to the same words; I do not want my man to compromise his principles.

"Go to the authorities and speak up for the right of widows to being a proud ex-wife of a service man, she should not be denied that right merely because of her changed social status. The authorities must recognise her being the closest support and motivation-to make him die for his nation. Let me tell you that all other factors of motivation to face the bullets encourages him to take on the little iron pieces in his chest. And, all that, you call her second hand. Please do something and be my real man."

Each word that she spoke had pierced my mind like a hot iron piece.

I realised that she was trying to prepare her soldier for a different battle.

8

Delayed Letter

On the thirteenth day of the war, our unit had captured the Alhar railway station of 'Pakistan-Western-Railways' on the Sialkot-Rawalpindi rail track. Our quartermaster, Captain Santokh Singh Dhillon, reported to me minutes after the capture. He was always very prompt to be with us and used to congratulate us personally after every assault and capture of a target. He was the unbreakable tail that was attached to the body of our unit. His responsibilities were to supply the troops with rations - water, arms, ammunition, clothing – as well as with many other necessities, including postal mail that he had received from the field post office.

On that day he gave me seven letters about the men of my company. I was very pleased to find a letter for Lieutenant Venu Gopal, who was my company officer.

At that time Lt. Venu was on a very important operational assignment. He had just captured the enemy post which was nicknamed 'Grove,' as the commander of one of my company's three platoons. The fighting was still continuing, and I was anxiously waiting for a message from him.

Just then my wireless operator gave me the handset and told me that Lt. Venu was on the air: "Tiger speaking, over."

"Heavy attack from West, out." Lt. Venu did not say anything else.

I signalled to my second-in-command to attack the enemy at their rear, from a direction to the west of Grove, and he did not waste a single moment to take off.

With one platoon I leapt up to Venu's position from the front and got engaged in hand-to-hand bayonet fighting. The enemy troops started retreating, but they were attacked from the rear by my second-in-command. Nearly one company strength of the enemy troops was wiped off.

My wireless operator started to tie a bandage on my left arm, as it was profusely bleeding, due to dagger injury. I found Lt. Venu lying in a pool of blood that was oozing out of his head and left arm. I rushed and lifted him with the help of my wireless operator and carried him to the nearest vehicle, where a few of our other injured boys were being carried for medical aid. Inside the moving vehicle, first aid was given to the injured. They were evacuated to the field ambulance medical unit.

We became occupied with reorganising ourselves. My injuries were not very deep, and I was happy with the first aid.

Lt. Venu suffered deep dagger injuries on his forehead and his left hand. He was declared out of danger four days after the operation, but before he was moved to the officers' ward of a base hospital, he was kept under observation in the intensive care unit for another three days.

The war ended on the twentieth day, and I visited Lt. Venu in the base hospital on the first occasion which I could manage. He had a bandage on his forehead covering both his eyes. His left hand had been amputated up to the wrist.

I moved to his bed and held his right hand. "How are you, Tiger?"

"Couldn't be better, sir." His voice was very strong.

I felt that his grip was harder than mine. Through the touch, we could feel each other's spirit.

"So how are the docs (doctors) treating you?" I asked.

"Oh, they are angels. I was told that they snatched me away from the clutches of *yamraj* (lord of death) by operating upon me for five hours continuously. Sometimes I wonder how these AMC people can manage to work so hard, with such a delicate job of cutting and stitching the inner organs of human beings. They are just great. Their dedication to their duties and their devotion goes without appreciation most of the time. Tell me, how are you, sir? I am told that you too had to shed lots of blood," he said.

"Not much. I am fighting fit. The old man is writing about you (making recommendations for a gallantry award). Subedar Chand Ram, Naib subedar Allah Baksh, Naik Swarn Singh and Sepoy S. P. Solanki have attained martyrdom. A few other boys were injured, but all are fit like a fiddle now. How are your eyes?" I asked.

"I don't know. Even the doctors do not know yet. They will find out when my bandage is removed. What else is the news?" he asked me.

"Yeah, there is something else. I have received a telegram that your elder brother together with your parents will arrive tomorrow to meet you," I told him.

"How did they come to know?" he asked.

"We sent them a telegram. I will go to meet them at the railway station. I have booked them in the rest house," I informed him.

"Oh, my mother will not be able to see me in this condition," he said.

"What are you talking? She has given birth to, and has brought up, a 'Tiger Son' like you, and you say that she would not be able to see you in this condition? In the telegram, your father wrote that they are proud of you and all of us who have shed blood for Bharat Mata. And, my dear friend, there is another good news for you - a letter from Rajani," I told him.

"What, what are you saying? A letter from Rajani? How is that possible? Did you send her a telegram too?" he asked me.

"No, she does not know that you have been injured. In fact I received this letter about twelve days ago, on the day when we captured the Alhar railway station. It was delivered to me one minute before you called on wireless from the Grove about the attack. This letter to you is rather delayed. Please forgive the delay in the delivery of the letter to you. You know how things were at that time," I said.

"No problem. But why should she write to me? I thought that she never wanted to have anything to do with me any more. You know it. I have told you everything. How did she come to think of writing to me after that serious fight which we have had last time? She told me that she had broken the relationship for ever," he said.

"You will know after you have read the letter," I gave him the letter. He kissed the envelope.

"But how can I read the letter? I don't know whether I will ever be able to read" He looked disappointed.

"Certainly you will be able to read the letter. Soldiers always think positive. Your eyes are alright. You were hit at the head. You will be absolutely alright, now that she is also come back to you. It is a sign of good luck," I said.

He said, "anyway, there is no use in talking about this subject before we know what she has written. She might have written to me to forget her. Please do me a favour and read the letter to me. I still cannot figure out what made her write to me. She was so angry when we met last. Wait a minute please .... . Sir, I hope that you have not written this letter yourself, on her behalf, just to please me. Sir, I cannot tolerate any sort of pity. I know you cannot see any body unhappy and would do whatever possible to make others happy. But kindly tell me the truth." He said.

"Venu, I must confess and tell you the truth. You see, when you told me about your deep love for her, and the fight that you have had with her, I could figure out that you were feeling very hurt, and that you were afraid of losing her. I felt that it would be very difficult for you. I felt very sad for you. I must make it clear to you that it was not with the aim to do you any favour, but to overcome my own uneasiness. I wrote a letter to Rajani in which I told her of your true love for her. Of course, I praised you as a wonderful man who loved her sincerely."

"You are great, sir, but I do not think that it was necessary to plead for her mercy, even though I know that a life without her is worthless."

"Not mercy. There is no question of mercy; it is just a simple question of placing the facts before someone without whom you cannot live. This was very necessary, before it was too late," I said

"Yeah, I understand; you are a very kind-hearted man and had to write what was necessary for my happiness. Please read the letter for me, sir," he requested.

I opened the letter and read.

"Dearest Venu, I am writing this letter in response to a letter that I have received from your company commander Major Teji. Firstly, please accept my sincere apologies for my behaviour when we met the last time. In fact, you were also very rude; but I should not have said what I said then. Please, please, please pardon me. I am very sorry.

"I realised the depth of my love for you after departing from you; and my ego did not allow me to write to you first. It was so kind of Teji to write me. It gave me courage to write back to you. I realise now that my love for you was for your inner personality, your soul. You see, initially we get attracted to our bodies to our looks. But true love develops when we recognise each others' inner personalities, when we can actually feel each others' souls. I confess, my love for you is from the core of my heart and soul.

"I must say that I would almost have lost you, if I had not received Teji's letter, or if it had been delayed by a few days.

"In fact my parents have been very eager for me to marry early. They introduced me to a few boys and were very keen on a particular one. I told them about my feelings for you. I said that I was in love with you and wanted to marry you. But they specifically asked whether you had proposed to me, which you have never done. They laughed off the matter with remarks of a fifty percent affair.

"Luckily my parents are very open-minded and want me to decide about my marriage myself. They have never interfered in my personal affairs. I so much wanted, and used to pray everyday, to get a letter from you. But you never wrote. I am sure that your ego stopped you from writing to me.

"It is so kind of Major Teji. He seems to be a man out of this world. I convey my sincere gratitude to him. I will always be indebted to him for giving you back to me.

"Venu, I appreciate the letter from Major Teji, but I sincerely wished in my heart of hearts that you had written to me that you loved me and wanted to marry me. Every girl yearns for a marriage proposal from the man, she loves.

"Yes, Venu, I openly say that I love you, and I hope you can hear the echo of my heart. See how fast it is beating. Can you hear the roar of the ocean?

Can you see the vast open sky which has no limits? And can you feel my love? I am sure you can. I wish, I hope, I pray.

"Now, you have to write to me. You must write to me. Propose to me. Will you? Be a good boy and act fast. I am ending this letter in a hurry, only to give you the chance to reply to me as soon as you can. Write to me now and immediately; otherwise I will feel that you do not love me at all. Venu, please write to me at once. Please propose to me by telegram.

"Yours forever, yours only and yours always,
Rajani."

Silence prevailed for some time. We were both thinking about the same thing. What now, after the injury?

I said, "Venu, you must write to her now."

"Do you think that she will have the same feelings after this injury?" He asked.

"Yes, I do think; rather I am confident that she will have the same feelings. You do not know the psychology of women. Once they are sincerely in love, they always remain faithful." I tried to sound convincing.

He said, "Sir, I think you have had a good experience in this field. Please, if you don't mind, tell me something about you," Lt Venu asked.

"What about me? There is nothing worth telling," I said.

He insisted, "no, sir, I always felt that you are not an average man. You cannot see anybody unhappy. You are always ready to help people in need. You are hiding some mystery in your mind. Your decision about not getting married in life and always trying to avoid topics concerning women has made others curious. We junior officers have often discussed that subject, but we could not find enough courage to talk to you. Sir, please tell me your story."

"My story? Yes, you are right; our past life becomes a story. The hard facts of someone's life might seem to be a mere fiction to the others. Those who try to laugh much might be trying to hide bundles of misery in their hearts. Anyway, if you insist, then I must tell you that my letter got delayed. That is all. It was my fault and I must suffer for that." I replied to him

"But, sir, is there nothing that can be done now?" He asked.

"No, there is nothing that can be done now. And there was nothing that could be done when my letter reached her. By then she was already married. My letter was delayed, too much delayed." I tried to bring the subject to an end.

"Sir, please do tell me in detail, if you don't mind. You will also feel better by talking about the past," he suggested.

I said, "her name was Agya Shukla. She stayed in my neighbourhood, and we had known each other since our childhood. We used to take good care of each other. It was like being in the habit of always caring for the other more than for oneself. I do not exactly remember when it happened, but by the time when we started our college studies, our friends had started to call us 'inseparables.' It all happened so gradually that we could never imagine any chance of separation. I think I took for granted that she understood my love, and I never realised that I should have made my love clear to her, and should have talked with her about marriage. Maybe I was over-confident of her. It always happens to the people who are the most intimate with each other that they take each other for granted.

"I come from a lower middle class family, and my first objective was to secure a respectable and well-paid career, so that I could offer a comfortable life to her, as my wife.

"I worked very hard and was awarded a scholarship for further studies in Chandigarh, which was 150 kilometres away from my hometown. In the meantime the government had declared Emergency Commission Service in the armed forces. I worked day and night to prepare myself and was selected to join the army as a commissioned officer.

After becoming an officer in the army I wrote to her that I was coming back home. But I was late, too late to miss all that for which I had been slogging all those years. I thought that I had reached my destination. But I never knew that I had taken the opposite direction and had actually reached the point of no return.

"When I reached home, my mother gave my letter back to me and told me that Agya had come to return that letter, and had said that she had waited for me for a very long time but had to agree to the pressure from her parents. She was married to an engineer in a wealthy and reputed family. She also had a small baby girl. She said that she would now have to wait for me until the next life.

Tell me, how can I get married during this life? We are both waiting. I must live my life to bear my punishment, and she must live her life to complete her duties. In fact, she is in a worse condition than I. She is living with the burden of many responsibilities, whereas I am living a free life."

"Sir, did you ever try to contact her after that?" he asked me.

"Was there any use in contacting her after that? In fact, that would have been my second big mistake. Indeed, creating social problems for someone you love is not only a mistake but a moral crime. My memories of her are most precious to me, and I would never let them fade away by meeting her and creating a flutter in her life," I said.

"I feel very sorry for you, Sir, and I sincerely hope that I can do something for you. Tell me, how can I repay you for what you have done for me?" he asked.

"There is nothing that you should do to repay me. I have done absolutely nothing for you. Nobody does anything for anybody else. In fact, when we do something for others, there may be only two main reasons. You are either doing favours in lieu of some obligations or to gratify your conscience in regard to those people. Take the example of parents when they bring up and look after their children; they are actually doing their duty which results from their natural love for them, and they perform certain social obligations. I wanted to eliminate my own uneasiness, because I felt that you were also about to meet a similar fate which would have brought misery to your life. I am feeling much more relaxed today. If you are very particular then my advice to you is to do the same again for someone else if you ever get an opportunity to do so," I told him.

I took leave from him with a promise to come back the next day with his parents.

The next day when I went to the railway station, I noticed a young girl with the parents of Lt. Venu. I introduced myself to them.

The father of Lt. Venu said, "meet my wife, my son and Venu's girlfriend Miss Rajani. When she learnt about Venu's serious injuries, she insisted on coming with us, and she said that it is the time when he needs her the most and that she would like to be with him. She really loves him very much. We are very pleased and proud to have her as a part of our family."

She came forward and touched my feet and said, "Uncle, it is because of Teji that I will be your daughter-in-law. My parents would have married me to someone else, because of some old misunderstanding between me and Venu, but this kind man wrote the facts to me in time, which saved the situation."

The old man came to me and held me in tight embrace for a while. We all went straight to the hospital. Everybody was happy to meet each other. Lt. Venu was discharged form the hospital after about two weeks. His eyes were perfectly alright. He was granted two months leave during which he got married to Rajani.

Some people are born lucky to enjoy their love life, but many others know how to make the best out of what life has to offer to them. Merely falling in love itself is a great matter of good luck. Once in love one can realise the exact value of life. Your mind can create the nectar of happy living if you sincerely try. You only have to be practical and positive in your approach and ready to compromise sincerely with the realities of nature.

9

The Enemy within the Country

My commanding officer had assigned to me a sacred duty of carrying and handing over the ashes of one of the soldiers of my platoon, who had attained martyrdom during the war, to the next of kin.

I had to complete the major part of my journey by train and the last ten kilometers of travel by bus, on bumpy tracks among the hills of Himachal Pradesh. So I had lots of time to think.

I started to reflect on my war experience. The soldiers who fought a war always considered themselves to be luckier than the others who did not get a chance to fight a battle during their tenure of service.

But, is it right to consider oneself lucky and to be proud of, taking part in the war? In the context of patriotism, maybe yes, but when viewed from a broader humanitarian perspective, war is a horrible truth. At times it is a necessary evil. It becomes necessary at a point of time when you cannot avoid it any further. Some people try to avoid it and others try to impose it. If you analyse history, most of the time you will find that the imposers became miserable cowards when they started losing their foothold or faced defeat. The truly brave heroes are often found in the category of peace-loving people.

If one wants any spell of peace to last, one has to accept war as a natural phenomenon. Hence it is always wise to be prepared to fight for the sake of peace. The destruction of life and the devastation which every war leaves in its wake, place the survivors in highly difficult situations. I am one of those who were destined to survive the war.

I reached the sleepy small village Paragpur, which is situated in the mountainous hinterland of Himachal Pradesh. There was only one mini-bus available which went to that village. It reached there in the evening and returned the next morning. So, there was no alternative but to stay there for the night.

By the time I reached the house the word had gone around that the ashes of Sepoy Sher Singh had arrived. Many of the villagers assembled in no time. Most of the younger lot wanted to ask me about the episode, but the elders told them to keep quiet for some time.

The young wife of the late Sher Singh let me inside the house and took me to another small room where an old lady was lying on the cot. She seemed sick and bed ridden.

"Have you arrived? You brought his ashes? Who are you?" said the old lady.

After paying my respects to her, I said, "*Mataji*, my name is Captain Paarth Arjun. I was his platoon commander. Sher Singh was a very brave soldier. Your son killed fifteen enemies and has won the battle, and he sacrificed his life for the sake of the nation as a great hero. He was really very brave. We all are very proud of him."

"What about you? Why didn't you sacrifice your life?" she asked.

Her daughter-in-law intervened. "*Mataji*, please stop it. He is a guest. It was none of his fault. It was our bad luck. It was destined to happen that way. Who could have helped?"

"See, who is defending you? She herself is defenceless - a young woman, who has got a long life to live, all alone.

How can she save herself from a society that looks down on the victims of bad luck? How can she protect her youth against the bad characters who keep hanging around from the so-called well-to-do and respectable houses? They blamed her for bringing bad luck to us.

"I told her father to take her back to his home but this unfortunate girl wants to stick around me. Her husband died doing his duty, and she wants to do her duty as well. To be good is always difficult. The poor girl does not realise that nothing is left of me. I am a guest for only a few days more. Maybe I will leave this world soon - I don't know. Why doesn't God take me from this world? His ways are strange. I do not understand. When it was time for me to depart, he took my young son away instead. There is no justice in His world. What can human beings do? Tell me, what have you done and what are you doing for us? she asked me. "Tell me, reply to me?"

"You will be paid a full pension for life, by the government," I said.

"Pension? Is that the full compensation for the life of a young man? What about the lives that he was supposed to support materially and socially? What about the security of his wife and her growing family? What are you doing for that? I told her father to take her away and marry her off to some other good young boy. He didn't do anything. Will you do that for her? Can you take her with you? Please take her away and find a companion for her. That would be better compensation," she pleaded.

I felt embarrassed and could not find the right words to reply to her. I found myself totally helpless.

"Look, *mataji*, I am not going with anyone. I have some obligations to you, and I am going to stay right here, with you. Don't worry, nothing will happen to me," the young woman said.

Right then, a man in his fifties came and said, "*Bhaudi* (sister-in-law), don't worry about her. I will take good care of her. My elder son can keep her. She will live comfortably in my house."

He signalled to all the villagers to go away. All the people vanished in no time.

"No, you get out of here, you scoundrel. Never dare to enter my house. I will kill you. Please *sahib*, tell this fellow to get out of my house. Please make him leave, at once." The old lady sounded very angry.

I looked at him with stern eyes.

"Okay, okay, it is alright, how long will this *sahib* save her from me. He will go away tomorrow. I will come back again. After all, we are also her relatives. We have rights in regard to her. Who would keep her, if not us? You die peacefully. Stop worrying about her." And he left.

Mataji told me, "this bad man is my husband's cousin brother. Tell me, how long I can save her from this rogue? He has bad intentions in regard to her."

"Is there no police here? What about the village Panchayat and other elders?" I asked.

"All are scared of him. He is a big *goonda* (bad character) and has been in jail before. He is a self-made 'village *mukhia*' (village head). The police station is ten kilometres from here. But they are seldom seen here.

"His eyes are on my little property and the pension which she would get for life. He does not want her to get married to anybody, because then she will lose the pension amount. He wants to keep her under his control as a 'keep,' so that he may get the pension as well as the property and can use her as a servant.

"My daughter-in-law is a very innocent girl. I want her to go away somewhere to live peacefully. Is there no place for her? Who will help her? How will she survive? Do something for her if your can. You say that army units are like close-knit families. What happens when one of your family members dies, especially when he dies for the sake of his country? You do nothing for him? Tell me, what are you doing for this unfortunate member of your family? Please help her. I don't want anything for myself. Take her with you. Can you do that?"

She kept repeating that until she fell asleep. The widow of Sepoy Sher Singh brought some food for me. I told her that I was not hungry and wouldn't eat anything. She showed me a cot to take rest. I lied down on the cot, but could not get any sleep. I found myself facing another war front - the enemies within the country. During battles in a war, all soldiers are prepared to die for each other. But here are the hapless close relatives of my fellow soldier, and they are in danger. Do I have any duty to them? What is my duty? What do I do?

I felt bad that I had fought the external aggressors for people like such traitors who have no conscience and would sell off their country for the lust of money. Such questions kept haunting me the whole night. I could not sleep a wink. I felt helpless, restless, and I kept changing my sides.

At about midnight I noticed the young woman standing next to my cot. She said, "*Sahib*, are you alright? You are not sleeping. Is anything wrong with you? Do you need any help?"

"Yes, I need help. I need to know what to do ... what to do about you ... how to protect you." I was angry with myself.

She said, "Don't worry about me. You have done your duty by bringing his ashes. Leave us to our fate. We will have to go through whatever is destined for us. Find some sleep. You have to travel tomorrow morning. You can do nothing."

I was struck by her last words. Is that true? Am I as incompetent that I could not have done anything for her? This felt like a big challenge for me. In fact, I have always been resentful of the word 'challenge.' It is one of my shortcomings since my childhood. Other boys used to take advantage of that weakness of mine.

Whenever they wanted to tease me or defeat me or humiliate me, they used to say that something was a 'challenge' for me. I always faced the 'challenge,' although many times I put myself in dangerous situations and lost the game. But accepting the challenges had become my passion. I asked her as to who else was in her family, and whether there was anyone on whom she could depend.

"Unfortunately, I have no other relative, only that uncle. My husband was the only child of his parents. In fact, I am not interested in the property. Let that go to them. The pension will be enough for me. I have an obligation to the mother of my husband, and for as long as she lives, I would stay with her, come what may. She tells me to go away, but I know that if I go away, she would die within a week if she was otherwise destined to live for six months. How can I leave her? Why should you trouble yourself for us? We live in a very small world. Jungle rule prevails here. Whatever uncle says is accepted by everybody. He has the power. He beats up the people who dare speak against him," she told me.

"What about the police?" I asked.

"The police station is very far away. The police never comes here. Two years ago the uncle has killed a young fellow in broad daylight, and the police did not come to know of it for six days. By then all the evidence had been destroyed. Everybody knew that the uncle was the killer. But nobody wanted to be the witness. Although he was taken into custody by the police, he came back within few months because the court had no evidence. Is it good for you that you do not involve yourself? You save yourself from that rascal and catch the morning bus. There is nothing that you can do," she said.

Was that true? I asked myself. Is that a fact that Captain Paarth Arjun, who was awarded the Veer Chakra by the President of India cannot do anything for the hapless family of one of his fellow soldiers? Can the family of brave soldier, who gave his life for the nation, be left to the mercy of a local bad character? What is my duty in this situation? Do I have any duty to them, official or moral? Does a moral duty give you the power to take any action?

The next morning I boarded the return bus. I noticed the wide-open blank eyes of the young widow watching me from the rooftop. Questions for me were written in her face, but no mercy appeal. About ten to twelve young villagers had gathered around the bus and were watching me with their disappointed eyes. More questions for me were written in their innocent eyes.

I got down from the bus and addressed them, "To be compelled to live in fear is a crime against humanity and against nature. Your village has produced a brave son in Sepoy Sher Singh, who fought single-handedly against fifteen armed and trained enemy soldiers and killed them. If your elders are scared it is for you young people to teach the culprit a lesson. I am told that he killed a friend of yours and you are keeping quiet?"

Suddenly one young boy came forward. "*Sahib*, he killed my elder brother and nobody helped us. I am very small now. Let me grow up; then I will kill that rascal. I will burn his entire family alive, one day. I will definitely do that ... ."

Another man came and started pulling him. "And before that he will kill you also. Do that when you grow up, but never utter a word now. Go to your house. You run away before he comes to know."

The boy ran away. That man came to me and said. "*Sahib*, you should leave now; otherwise the situation will take an ugly turn. Leave us to the mercy of the Lord."

I said, "You seem to be a wise man. Why don't you do something and bring this man to book. Find some witnesses for the murder that he has committed. Go to the police and to the court. I don't want to take law into my hands, otherwise I would ... ."

The driver came and advised me, "*Sahib*, please don't say anything more. We know that you can teach him a lesson. These villagers can be incited to revolt. They are already agitated and burning from inside, but that will only result in more bloodshed. Hence let us leave, please, *sahib*." And he caught my hand and almost pulled me inside the bus.

The bus started, and I found myself being dragged away. I felt sorry for the villagers and especially for the two ladies. Many questions kept haunting me. I could not sit in the bus for a long time. So I got down at the place where the police station was located.

On that day, the SHO had gone to the district court to attend a case. I introduced myself to the senior police inspector who was the additional SHO. He listened to me and told me that no offence has been committed so far; hence there was no case. So, they could take no action. The court had already acquitted him of the murder charge.

I was surprised by the role of the police, which has to wait until a crime has been committed. Only then can they bring the culprits to book. It is only a corrective action. Shouldn't society impose on them powers and responsibility for the prevention of the crime?

I felt disappointed and returned to my unit. I told the whole episode to my company commander, Major Sangram Singh, who took me to the CO (commanding officer) with whom we then discussed the whole case. The CO advised me to relax and concentrate on my unit routine work. In the evening I did not go to the officers' mess for food.

My company commander came to my room and asked, "are you alright? What is bothering you? Young man, your face looks as you have been crying. Tell me, what happened?"

"Sir, the close relatives of one of our dear soldiers are in danger. Can we not do anything? I am all the more shocked because my CO also took the things lightly and did not do anything. I am burning from inside. What should I do?" I asked.

He replied, "I know that you are a good man and that is why you are feeling the pain of others. When the bug of social injustice bites any noble one, for the sake of the victims, he cannot take rest. He loses his appetite and sleep. Just think of the Lord Jesus Christ. What sufferings did he have to bear and how much blood did he shed for the sake of innocent human beings who were the victims of social injustice. And Bapu Gandhiji? Imagine the misery that he had to suffer and all the sacrifices that he had to make. They also had to fight a war. This is not a soldiers' battlefront. This is not an easy war. Here the enemies are hidden within your own people. In this case your mechanical weapons are of no use. The point is not to eliminate bodies. Here the enemy is the social evil. Many a time, even the law of the land is ineffective. Have patience and faith in the 'Old Man'. You know him. I am confident that he will do something. Get dressed to go to the mess and have your food. Do you understand that? By remaining hungry you cannot help solve the problem. That cannot help them. Please have your food, brother. And if you don't listen to my advice, I will have to order you to consume the food. Is that clear? Any doubts?"

"No, sir," I said

He hugged me. I noticed that his eyes had become wet. Perhaps he had also been bitten by the 'bug.' I didn't know how much poison had spread.

After a few days we had our monthly Sainik Sammelan. All officers, JCOs and *jawans* had assembled in the large sports stadium. In the Sainik Sammelan anybody could raise any point of grievances of a general nature and the CO always made decisions on the spot.

Our CO said, "my dear officers, JCOs and *jawano*; you all have earned a good name for the unit by your brave actions of glory during the war. The nation has patted you on your backs by conferring gallantry awards on some of you. But I know that each one of you is brave as the other. I know that it is a fact because I have seen all of you fighting with dedication. These awards are for all of you, for the whole of my unit.

Listen to me carefully. I am giving an order to all of you at this moment. From now on, whenever you refer to our unit and mention the word 'unit,' you will utter the words 'My Unit.' Never say the word unit by itself. Always say 'my unit,' so that you can feel proud of yourself. Your chest should heave with pride when you utter the words 'my unit'. And whenever any member of 'my unit' is hurt, everyone of you should feel the pain. Is that clear?" My CO roared.

"Yes, sir," we all roared back.

He continued, "today I am throwing another challenge to you. I want to see all who are true sons of their mothers and who would voluntarily, without any sense of compulsion and obligation, be prepared to accept that challenge. But before I announce that challenge I want you to hear patiently what our Captain Paarth Arjun, Veer Chakra, has seen when he was sent to the village of our respected soldier Sher Singh to deliver his sacred ashes to his next of kin. Captain Paarth Arjun, get up and tell everybody what you have told me."

I got up and said, "respected CO, sir, my senior officers, and dear friends; I carried the sacred ashes of Sepoy Sher

Singh's departed soul to his small village in the remote area of Himachal Pradesh. When I got there I met his old, sick and bed-ridden mother and his young widow, who is about twenty years old. There is no other member in his family. These two ladies are living under the constant threat from and fear of the uncle of Sepoy Sher Singh, who wants to grab their property and keep the young girl under his control, so that he can continue to get the family pension. He does not want this girl to get married and escape from his clutches. The mother of Sepoy Sher Singh is a very pious and noble lady.

She wants to save the girl from that rogue. I spoke to the people of that village, but all are scared of him. I also went to the police station. But the police are not able to help because they say that the law does not permit them to take any action until a crime has been committed. I have done my duty of reporting the matter to my commanding officer." And I sat down.

The CO got up and said, "now the time for taking the challenge has come. I say again that I am not pressing anybody. I want truly willing and unmarried people who are sincerely prepared to get married to that young widow and also to look after the sick old lady. All those who would do that can now get up and raise their hands."

Almost fifty percent of the whole unit of about nine hundred people got up and raised their hands.

The CO said, "Good, bloody good. Well done. You are the cream of humankind and brave soldiers of my unit. I am really proud of you all. But there is another problem now. Who will select the most eligible groom among these approximately four hundred people?"

My company commander got up and said, "Sir, there is no need for any selections. The most eligible groom is also standing with his hands up, Captain Paarth Arjun, Veer Chakra."

Everybody started looking towards me. They all started clapping. My CO came to me and took me in his tight, affectionate embrace.

He started addressing all of us again. "This unique example of bravery and kindness will be written in the golden words of my unit's history. Today you have all set a great and noble example of human virtue. Well done, my boys. Let me tell you some more details. Yesterday I spoke on telephone to the deputy commissioner of police of that district. He has promised me immediate police protection for the ladies. He is also ready to re-open the case of murder against that culprit if anybody is prepared to present evidence or any witness.

I have deputed my Subedar Major Saheb and another JCO to go and meet the mother of Sepoy Sher Singh and the father of the girl, and if they agree we will all become *baraati* (marriage party) for the great occasion. Does anybody want to say something? Are there any doubts?"

"No, sir," the whole unit got up to greet the 'Old Man.' The whole area echoed with our unit slogan and '*Jai Hind*.'

Our Subedar Major returned after about ten days. He informed us that the culprit had been arrested on a charge of murder. The whole village had become the witness to the crime. Finally peace and harmony returned to that village.

The mother of late Sepoy Sher Singh and the father of the young girl were greatly pleased to know about the marriage proposal.

I felt that I had won the battle.

10

Love Triangle

I knew Major Sampuran Singh from my school and college days where he was one year senior to me. He was an excellent sportsman, but not very good at studies. He joined the army two years before me, as I had wasted one year studying engineering and had only then changed over to join the services. He was called by his nickname "Punnu." Both of us were serving in the same unit.

Major Punnu was a great lover of the nature. Any beautiful thing touched him easily. Charming scenery, beautiful flowers, the smile of a child, good poetry, soothing music, or any other such thing would touch his heart and bring tears of joy to his eyes. He used to watch the activities of nature with intense concentration.

He used to say, "These are proofs of the existence of the God Almighty. He exhibits Himself in abundance. His presence can be felt equally well in the smallest atom and in the limitless sky. I cannot imagine that there are human beings who do not believe in the existence of God. I feel justified to call such people fools, or at least ignoramuses."

I always admired him as a good human being for that quality, but I wondered whether that made him a good soldier. We often had long discussions on the topic. Once, during one such casual discussion, he mentioned that one day he would die a beautiful death.

I got annoyed and told him that he was defining the darkness as a bright white light. Death can never be beautiful. Many a time I viewed him like an innocent child. His decisions were also very quick. At times he would suddenly give out his decision and stick to it.

Once during our annual leave, when both of us had gone for a walk in our town's district park, he suddenly caught my hand with a very hard grip and said, "See ... look at that girl. I have never seen a more beautiful woman than her in my life. God must have created her when He was at His best in His creative effort."

I saw tears in his eyes. I knew what had happened to him.

"Why? Do you really think she is that beautiful?" I asked.

"Yes, yes, yes, the most beautiful girl I have ever seen. Oh God, how do you do that? Why do you do that? You display the beauty only for a second. Why can't you hold on for the onlooker to let him appreciate your creation fully? I know she will vanish before I have seen enough of her," he said.

"Oh, poet *sahib*, please stop. What are you saying? I do not understand anything. Are you serious?" I asked.

"Oh yes, I am very serious. I have fallen in love with her. This is called love at first sight. I wish I could marry her. God promise."

"How can you talk like this? You are a mad man. What if she is already married? How can you think such things? You saw a girl and want to marry her. You do not know anything about her, and you say that you want to marry her." I was totally annoyed with him.

"Please Munnu, please do not talk to me like my father. Help me if you can. At least find out her address before she goes away," he pleaded.

Suddenly I realised that he was very serious. I headed straight for that girl. I found that there was an old man with her. His face seemed to be familiar to me.

I said, "Good morning, sir, I believe you know my father, Shri Jiwan Mohan?"

"Oh yes, of course I know your father. In fact, we are very close friends. Have you come on leave? The other day he was telling me that you are likely to come on leave. How are you?" He asked.

"Fine, thank you, sir. May I know your good name, sir?" I asked.

"My name is Des Raj Gupta. Have you come on annual leave? How long are you going to be home? Meet my daughter, Rachna. She has completed her graduation this year," he said.

"Hello ... ." I realised that she was indeed very beautiful.

After a few courtesies, I excused myself and went straight to Punnu. "Eh man, just remember the names of Mr. Des Raj Gupta and his daughter Rachna. The old man is a friend of my father. I will try to arrange a meeting."

"Oh Munnu, I will always be grateful – rather, indebted – to you if you arrange my marriage with her. Please, Munnu, do this for me." He again pleaded. I knew it was useless to argue with him. Later when I met my father I enquired about Rachna and her father.

"Why, have you met her?" he asked.

"Yes, her father was also with her." I told him.

"Do you like her? In fact your mother and I like her very much. Rachna's father too has expressed similar views about you, and he has even spoken to Rachna as well about her marriage to you. She has also agreed. Now it all depends on you. We have decided to celebrate your engagement with her during this leave. I am glad that you met her," my father said.

"But daddy; my friend Major Punnu likes her and wants to marry her," I told him.

"But we have already decided your marriage with her," said my father.

"No, that is not possible. What would my friend think of me? He loves her, daddy, and you have to help me to arrange his marriage with her. And if you do not do that, I will talk to them and tell them that I do not like her." I gave my final decision.

Suddenly my father became serious. The elders discussed the matter, and Punnu was married to Rachna.

It was at 1:00 a.m. in the night after their marriage when I was woken up by loud knocks at the door. I opened the door and found Punnu standing there.

"What the hell are you doing here? It is your honeymoon night and you have come to me? Why, what happened?" I asked.

"I have come to thank you friend. Rachna has told me everything ... that her marriage had already been fixed with you. What a beautiful example of true friendship. You have to come with me right now. We both must thank you, Munnu," he said.

It took me a great effort, and a promise to have breakfast with them the next morning, to persuade him to go back.

On 3 September 1965, one year after their marriage, the war with Pakistan started. Rachna was five months pregnant then.

Major Punnu was the company commander in our unit. His personal example of leading the troops during the assaults and as an untiring, patriotic soldier had motivated his troops to a very high degree. Major Punnu had earned the reputation of being a terror for the enemy. Our battalion had done remarkably well during the war.

The ceasefire was declared on 23 September and was to be effective from midnight. The agreement of both the governments was that the troops were to settle down wherever they were just then and that firing would stop at midnight. No forward movement was to take place after that time. Troops were to take positions wherever they were at that moment.

On the early morning of the next day, I heard Major Punnu talk to the CO. Major Punnu informed the CO that after the ceasefire limit had expired, the enemy had crept up and occupied some land in front of his company's location. He was seeking permission to push the enemy back. But the commanding officer explained to him that we have to honour the ceasefire agreement. No action could be taken.

After some time, we suddenly heard small arms firing and the unit came instantly to 'stand to' (ready to retaliate). Later it was found that Major Punnu had attacked the defaulting enemy, killing thirty one enemy troops. Major Sampuran Singh, along with five Jawans, had attained martyrdom.

Thus the great lover of nature and the one who loved life most, embraced his beautiful death. I could not quite understand how all that had happened so suddenly.

I found myself confused and could not find answers to many questions. My friend who used to consult me about even the most minor issues took the greatest decision of his life without even mentioning it to me? Did his life belong to him only? Why did he not realise that many other lives were connected and dependent on him?

Was this the end of the story? No, that was certainly not the end of story. Death can end a life, but it cannot end the story of that life because every life starts the stories of many other lives. In this case the lives of his wife and her unborn child were directly affected.

I learnt that Sepoy Abdul Ghani had gone to the commanding officer the very next morning and had argued with him to launch an attack on the enemy immediately.

The CO tried to pacify the soldier in simple words and explained to him that the firing had been stopped on the orders from higher authorities and that no action should be taken to break the promise of the government.

"But, sir, our brave Major *sahib* is lying on the land of the enemy, and we cannot do anything? When the enemy has broken the agreement, we should certainly give a fitting reply. Please give us the orders to attack," He tried to reason.

The commanding officer said, "Sepoy Abdul Ghani, do not argue with me. You should not see with the point of view of the enemy. You should see your own point of view and act. We Indians are known to say "*Jaan jai, par wachan na jai*" (Lose your life but not your word). Always remember that and go back and do your duty."

"Yes Sir I will do my duty," he saluted and went away.

After about an hour we heard sounds of firing again. This time, the loyal soldier of his company commander, Sepoy Abdul Ghani, had attacked the enemy single-handedly and had killed two enemy troops before attaining martyrdom. The great '*Sahayek*' joined his officer on the never-ending route-march.

Time continued its journey. I did not realise that the second anniversary of my friend's death had arrived. In the meantime, Rachna had given birth to a baby girl who was by now one and a half year old and had started balancing her steps on earth.

Throughout this entire period I felt guilty for having forced her to marry Punnu, only to become a widow ultimately. My parents advised me many times to get married, but I tried to change the topic every time. I made up my mind not to get married, and if I had to bow to their pressure at all, then I should propose to Rachna.

My mother insisted that I accompany my parents to Rachna's house to pay homage to the departed soul on his death anniversary. I hesitated at first, but then I acquiesced to the wishes of my parents.

On the way, my mother said, "Son, we must think of Rachna. She has a along life to live. We must accept the fact that destiny has made us the cause of her misfortune. Therefore it is our duty to do something for her."

"What do you have in mind, mother"? I asked.

"Son, in our religious teachings, the second marriage of a young widow is advised." She said.

"I understand what you are trying to say, mother, and I agree that you are right. But what Rachna thinks is the most important thing. Would she agree in the present circumstances? I am ready only if Rachna agrees," I replied

"Thank you, son. In fact the elders, including her parents and her in-laws, have already discussed the matter and have given their consent. We were waiting to hear about your wishes. Rachna is a wise girl. She does not hold anyone responsible for whatever has happened. She believes that perhaps the Almighty had planned it that way." My mother patted me on my back.

I got married to Rachna after a few months. On the first night, when I entered the dimly-lit bedroom, I found Rachna sitting on a corner of the bed, almost bundled up in heavy garments and jewellery.

"Why is the bed empty, Rachna?" I asked.

"I do not understand. What do mean?" She said.

"I mean, where is my Munny? Let me make it clear at this stage that she is the most precious gift that you have given to me and she must sleep with her parents." I said.

"Yes, darling, she will sleep with her parents, but not tonight. Tonight is their *suhaagraat*. She will sleep with her parents from tomorrow onwards. Is that okay with you?" She caught my hand.

"Yes, darling, it is okay with me." and the story continued with another pleasant turn.

11

Sainik Veer Singh

Sainik Veer Singh was my *sahayak* (helper) before and during the war. He was a serious type of person who did not like to talk much and used to keep to his job only. He could be described as a real professional soldier. During the war, he was with me in all the assaults.

He would never get tired of digging the trenches or lifting battle equipment. He was very alert on sentry duties, and – when the other sentry fell sick or had another problem - volunteered most often to stand in for him.

He had a small family - his mother, his wife and an eight years old daughter. He used to talk to me about his family, and especially about his mother.

His father had sacrificed his life during the previous war and was decorated with "Veer Chakra." That is why he was named Veer Singh.

Once he told me that during his last leave, his mother had put the 'Veer Chakra' medal on her forehead and instructed him thus: "son, please put this medal on my forehead when I die so that I look "*suhagan*." This incident, as well as many others, showed how patriotic his mother was. His wife and daughter also loved the motherland very much. At least that is what Veer Singh used to say. He told me about certain miracles that had been performed by his mother.

Sometimes I wondered whether all what he said about his mother was correct. He almost worshipped his mother and always carried her photograph in his pocket.

Once, before the war, at the peace station, he went to see his mother without obtaining proper leave, and he was punished. He had no regrets about his act and never asked for a pardon, because he agreed that it was an offence to go on leave without leave. He explained that he had dreamt that his mother was very sick, and there was not enough time left to catch the next train. Such was his obsession about his mother.

Once he asked me to read a letter that his little daughter had written to him during the war days. She had written, "Bapu (father), you must have killed many enemies. Bring some of their skulls. Those skulls should be large enough to be houses for all the mice that live in our fields. The mice have spoiled the crops. I will bury those skulls in our fields, so that all the mice can live there. Mummy says that you can come home only when the war ends. We are very fine. Don't worry about us. I am looking after grandma. She is fine. I go to the temple with her everyday to pray for your victory. What medal will you win? Bring Param Veer Chakra. I like Param Veer Chakra."

He also showed me another small note that was written by his wife and had been enclosed with his daughter's letter. "Pritam (darling), *mataji* is fine, and she sends her blessings to you. We look after her. You do your duties well, like your father."

On the eighth day of war I was to lead my platoon to an assault on an enemy post which was located on a hillock. Although there were no hills in that sector, there was a small mound which we had named 'Tekri'. The enemy had a dominant position on that post, from where intense fire could be brought down on our advancing columns. We had the information that a one company strength of the enemy was occupying the mound and the slopes.

Had it been a day attack, we would have requested air-support or bombing by the artillery. But there are many occasions when there is no time to wait for support firing. My CO ordered me to charge from the right flank. It was a pitch-dark night, and there was no other way but to crawl up the hill.

I positioned myself at the leading point and placed my boys on arm's length, both on my right and left. We had agreed on the signal of touching each other's arm after crawling up five steps, so that we would not lose the direction or miss each other. Similarly, other troops were to follow us in a more dispersed configuration. My advancing column made a arrow shape. Two other platoons of our company were to crawl up in a similar manner and configuration, from the front, keeping a distance of five steps behind our position. We were to maintain complete silence to achieve total surprise. Our only means of communication was touch at regular intervals of five steps. Until the time when everybody had received that signal, nobody was to take any further step. We were moving up as though we were a mechanical body as one set.

When I had come within about five feet of the enemy's machine gun position, from where I could jump and pounce upon the enemy, I fired a varilight shot. Then about another ten varilight pistols were fired by our other designated troops immediately after my shot. The entire area was lighted up. We made a final attack on the unaware enemy, and our attack was followed by fighting with daggers and bayonets and small arms.

"*Bacho, sahibji*" (save yourself, sir), I heard Veer Singh say; and with that he pushed me on one side. I turned immediately; and I found that Veer Singh had taken the dagger blow on himself and was about to fall down.

I caught his limp body in my arms. By this time the whole of our battalion was on the top of the hill, and we had killed about forty enemy soldiers while others had fled.

Soon we reorganised ourselves and took up new defensive positions where only a few minutes earlier enemy soldiers had been sitting. All our casualties were evacuated to the field ambulance medical unit.

Sainik Veer Singh was unconscious for two days, but fortunately he was declared out of danger after an operation. He, along with our other seriously wounded comrades, was shifted to the army base hospital.

Soon after the ceasefire had been declared, I went to see him in the base hospital. He tried to get up to greet me, but I hugged him on his bed and held him for some time. This was our way of thanks giving, as the soldiers never say "Thank you" in spoken language.

"*Mataji* saved us," Veer Singh said.

I was again reminded of his mother, and that increased my curiosity to meet her.

During my next annual leave I went to his village and visited his family. The child was very happy with the gifts which I had taken for her. I touched the feet of his mother. She was a simple lady, and she was completely illiterate. She was very happy to meet me and enquired about her son Veer Singh.

"He is fine and remembers you all very much."

"Tell us something about the war," asked her mother.

I narrated many incidents to them, and they listened with much interest. His daughter asked me many questions, to which I replied with great care.

"How do you get time to remember your family members during the war? His father never remembered us when he fought the war."

"For remembering anybody, we do not have to leave our physical work. It is a fact that Veer Singh remembered you at all times. In fact, he praises you very much; rather, he worships you and says that you have some divine powers."

"*Pagla hai* (he is mad). He should take me as his mother rather than make a goddess out of me," she said.

"But there must be some reason why he believes you as a Goddess," I said.

"Yes, there is a reason. But still, I do not deserve what he thinks about me. You see, I brought him from an orphanage when he was six years old and adopted him as my son. He knows that circumstance and feels that I did him a great favour. In fact, I am indebted to him because he has made me a mother. My daughter-in-law joined my family because of him and I was blessed with my granddaughter because of him. It means that he gave me much more than I gave him. He is the best son in the whole world. I do not want a devotee. I want a son, and I wish that he would take me as his mother. *Sahibji*, you are his commander. At least you can help me to get my son back."

"Yes, I will certainly try my best, and I will advise him as you want." Then I took my leave from them.

12

Human Sacrifice

We were deployed somewhere in the Poonch sector of Jammu and Kashmir state on the Pakistan border. It was a mountainous terrain with numerous small and big hills and thick jungles on the slopes. The border was actually the line of control, consisting of army posts located at the hill tops.

My company was located on a hillock which dominated the area. It is a big strategic advantage for any unit to be on the dominating position. We could clearly see some of the enemy posts and surrounding locations.

At times, the enemy would suddenly start firing artillery shells, mainly with a view to inducting infiltrators, or when one of their VIPs visited the border area. We were well aware of their designs and immediately took counter measures to thwart their intentions. This had become almost routine practice.

The village 'Allah Rakha Haji Peer Wale' was located at the foot of our hill. In that village, there was the *dargah* of Haji Peer Baba (the holy tomb of a Mohammedan saint). We learnt that the *dargah* was more than one hundred years old.

In fact, this dual name of the village was strange. The first portion of the name, Allah Rakha, had been added to the old name of Haji Peer Wale about four years earlier. It so happened that at that time, as the villagers celebrated

Peer Baba Day, an army unit of the enemy infiltrated during the night and attacked the village, with a view to capture the strategically significant hill.

At that time, there existed a small Indian army post which consisted of a section with only eleven men. *Havildar* Allah Rakha of that section displayed exemplary courage; he pushed back the enemy, inflicting nine casualties on them, and he thus saved the village. Since then the people started calling the village by its present dual name.

Many stories were connected to the 'Haji Peer Baba. People firmly believed that whosoever came to the *dargah*, his wishes were fulfilled. One such story was that during the *mela* (fare), which was held once in every four years, Haji Peer Baba accepted a sacrifice of human life. Pilgrims used to come from near and far to pay their homage on the festival day.

Our unit had adopted that village for social welfare and medical aid schemes. The name of the village *Mukhia* (headman) was Abdul Kareem, and he was of a highly religious bent. All the villagers had lot of respect for him.

Whenever any defence personnel visited our post, they always paid their respects at the *dargah*. We provided all the necessary aid to the holy shrine. We had dug down trenches and bunkers at the slopes and on the hill and had made proper defensive positions. Our sentries were alert around the clock. We, all officers and other ranks, used to live on that big mountain.

At about 4:00 p.m. on one afternoon, suddenly, a small girl came running into my bunker, shouting "Abbu, Abbu (daddy)."

I was taken aback and shouted for the sentry in order to find out how the small girl could have reached my bunker. He replied that he had tried to stop her, but had not fired as she was just a small child.

The child said, "Abbu, do not shout at him. I came on my own to meet you."

"Who Abbu? Who is your Abbu? Who sent you here?" I asked her.

"Nobody. I have come to meet you, *Abba.*" She started crying bitterly.

"Don't cry, calm down, please be quite. What is your name?" I tried to calm her down.

"Naheed. Abba, you forgot my name?" She sounded surprised.

"Where do you live? Who came with you?" I asked.

"Nobody, Abbu. Why don't you live with us, Abbu? Now I will live with you here. I will not go to *Ammi.* She is very bad. She does not let me meet you," the little girl said. By then my second-in-command, Captain Amar Jit had arrived, and he tried to pull my leg. "Sir, you have kept this secret from us. I think, I should immediately inform *bhabhiji* (my wife) about this secret affair."

"Oh, you shut up. Go to the village and find out whose child she is. And take her with you, will you? Quick, go, take off." I ordered him.

Captain Amar Jit was about to leave when we heard our sentry shouting, "*Thum, koun ata hai? Haath uppar.* (Stop. Who is there? Hands up.)"

We both came out and saw that a woman with her hands up was standing about twenty five yard away on the down slope.

"Who are you?" I asked.

"*Janab* (sir), my name is Reshma. I live in the village down there. My daughter has come here. I have come to take her back," she replied.

I asked her to come up, "tell me, what is all this?"

"Janab, my husband was once in charge of this post. He sacrificed his life when he was posted here, four years ago. My daughter does not understand that and she always cries to meet him. I lied to her that her father lives on top of the hill, believing that she would never be able to climb up. I always keep her locked up inside the room. But today she escaped and climbed up. Please let us go," she pleaded.

"What was the name of your husband?"

"Havildar Allah Rakha. The village has been named after him," she replied.

I asked one JCO (junior commissioned officer) to go to the village and call the *Mukhia*.

"Why does she call me Abba?" I asked.

"Janab, a few days ago you had come to visit the village. She saw you from the rooftop and asked me whether you were her Abba. To placate her, I said yes, and since then she has become very hysterical and wanted to see you," she said.

After some time, the Mukhia came. I told him about the entire incident and asked him about the woman.

"Janab, Reshma is the daughter of my late sister, and she teaches in our village primary school. She was married to Havildar Allah Rakha who was once serving on this post. Her husband was very brave. Four years ago, when the enemy attacked us, he saved the village and this hill, and he sacrificed his own life. She is a very good lady, and she teaches for free in the village primary school. Please permit us to leave."

I offered them tea and snacks. Before leaving, the *Mukhia* said, "Janab, I have a small request. Tomorrow is Peer Baba's day. There will be a good *Qawwali* programme. Please come to the *dargah*."

But Reshma interrupted, "Mama (uncle), have you forgotten what happened four years ago on this very day?"

"Oh yes, yes.... She is right, Janab please do not come. On this day, four years ago, the enemy has attacked our village. Please be extra careful tomorrow. God be with you. We take leave." They all left.

I called an immediate meeting of my subordinates and briefed them about the position. And I ordered them to be very cautious. I informed my headquarters also. We sent reconnaissance patrolling parties in the evening on both days.

At about 11:00 p.m., our forward sentry pulled a cord which I had kept tied to my leg for any emergency warning. I crawled up to him. He pointed out to a bush from where a faint light was being flashed at short intervals. Thinking that it was a friend, I said "come up" at a volume which could only reach up to the bush.

I noticed a figure slowly climbing up. When the person came nearer, I recognised that it was Reshma. She ran straight into my bunker. She was breathing heavily. I offered her a glass of water.

She said, "Janab, I have noticed some people gathering in a suspicious manner, and I am wondering whether they are enemy troops. Be careful."

I immediately made a bird's sound which signalled to everyone to come to "stand to" (absolute readiness to retaliate).

We all took our positions, got glued to the ground and started observing our front and flanks. After some time I saw through my infra-red binocular that a few figures were crawling up. According to a pre-decided signal, I fired a varilight shot, and immediately after that, my second-in-command fired few more vary-light shots. We pounced on the enemy with heavy fire. For some time, the hills kept roaring with the deafening sound of gunfire. Heavy firing from enemy posts also continued.

In the meantime a re-enforcement from our battalion had also arrived. My commanding officer had reached my location within a very short time of the first shot having been fired, and the whole operation was conducted on his orders. He told us to intensify the firing and keep up the pressure. We dispatched a few patrols to kill if any enemy soldier whom they might encounter and also to asses the strength of the enemy. By five o' clock in the morning the patrols confirmed that there was no enemy anywhere except on their normal posts.

We continued the firing until first light. After daybreak, our fresh patrols had combed the entire area and informed us that there were ten dead bodies of enemy soldiers lying on the slopes of our hill.

We noticed a white flag on the nearest enemy post. This meant that they were requesting a ceasefire and a flag meeting, and this was subsequently held.

I went down to the village with Reshma and met the Mukhia, and I told him, "Sir, like her brave husband four years ago, your niece has saved the village on this auspicious day of Peer Baba. And as far as the human sacrifice is concerned, we have killed ten enemies. Hence Peer Baba should be pleased not to take any more sacrifices for another forty years.

"*Inshah* Allah," said the *mukhia*.

13

Let Love Be the Winner

During the War, our battalion had earned a good name. We had won a good number of gallantry awards. In the unit's roll of honour, and among the soldiers who had brought pride to the unit, the name of Sainik Sameer Das Gupta had found a respectable place.

He was one of the most courageous soldiers of our unit. Most of the time, he had volunteered to go on patrol or to act as a scout. Such duties were physically and mentally strenuous, because they involved collecting as much accurate information about the enemy positions as possible by going very close to them. He used to derive pleasure from such adventures and used to call them as 'outings'.

After the war, our unit had moved back to the location of the old peace station. Sainik Sameer Das Gupta was awarded the Sena Medal, and the award ceremony was still due to be held. In the meantime, a very embarrassing situation had arisen. Sameer had gotten involved in a minor disciplinary case. Looking at his old records the commanding officer gave him a verbal warning and advised him not to repeat the incident.

The next morning, he was found missing from the unit lines, and he was eventually apprehended at the railway station. Once again, our CO did not take a very serious view and, keeping in view his past gallantry record, issued him the last warning.

Normally, pardons are not granted in disciplinary cases, because the army act is very strict. However, the old records of the soldier were exemplary; hence the CO gave him another chance.

After a few days, he applied for leave, and he also told his immediate senior rank that he would go on leave but would not come back. It was a surprising and serious matter. I was instructed by my CO to discover the facts.

I spoke to him, "Sameer, you are a good soldier. The commanding officer has been very kind to you and has pardoned you twice. I have been told that you have said that you would go on leave but would never come back."

"Yes, sir. I have said that." He replied.

"But why did you say that? Do you know that it is a matter of indiscipline, and you can be punished for that? In any case, under the present circumstances, you will not be granted leave," I told him.

"But, I will still go," he said.

"You cannot. And let me tell you that I can put you in quarter guard (army lock-up) for saying what you have said to me just now," I warned him. He kept quiet.

"Do you understand what I have told you, and can you tell me what has happened to you? You are such a nice guy, and you are behaving like this!? I do not understand what has happened to you. Who is misguiding you? You would be the biggest fool to behave like this. You know that the Sena Medal has been awarded to you. Such high honour has been bestowed upon you because you have been a good disciplined soldier and have shown exemplary courage in the face of the enemy. It is a matter of great pride for any soldier. Come on, tell me what is wrong with you! Take me as your elder brother. I will help you. I want to help you. You have displayed so much courage during the war. You have brought pride to the unit. You are a disciplined soldier. You cannot behave like this. Do you understand?" I asked him.

He moved his head in affirmation and went back to his barrack. I instructed my senior JCO to keep an eye on him and also to find out why he suddenly started behaving like that, and whether someone was misguiding him. It was a mystery to me.

On the next day the senior JCO came to me and gave me a closed envelope which was addressed to Captain Sameer Das Gupta. I called Sameer and gave him the letter; and I asked him whether it was his letter. He confirmed that the letter belonged to him.

"Why is 'Captain' mentioned next to your name? Are you a captain?" I asked.

"No, sir." He replied.

"Why is the rank of Captain mentioned alongside your name? Come on, reply to me!" I directed him.

He said, "I do not know, sir. Someone must have written it just like that."

"And who is this someone? Do you know that it is a crime not to give your correct rank? It amounts to fraud." He kept quiet.

"Come on, speak out, say some thing, damn it." I was annoyed.

He did not say anything. I tried to bring it out from him, but he did not utter a word. I found the case slightly delicate. In the armed forces, punishing a subordinate is very easy, because the officers have the powers of the judiciary. But the present case was quite peculiar, because this behaviour was not expected of the person in question. I sent him to the unit lines and instructed the senior JCO to go into the depth of the matter and find out the exact problem. Knowing of his brave acts of valour during the war days, I was not prepared to accept that suddenly he had become an undisciplined soldier. His behaviour seemed to me like that of an adamant child who would deliberately resort to naughty acts to tease his elders. I was convinced that there was something seriously wrong with him.

After a few days, I was informed that Sainik Sameer had applied for discharge from service about two months earlier. Looking at his service records, it was explained to him that he had a bright career to look forward to and that he should reconsider his decision. His application was not forwarded. Lately he had been getting a lot of correspondence. Most of his letters are addressed to him as Captain Sameer Das Gupta. He seems to be suffering from depression and anxiety. He insisted on being discharged immediately.

In the next few days I had to go on temporary duty to an outstation. When I came back I was told that he was locked up in quarter guard. I was the duty officer for the day and was informed that Sainik Sameer Das Gupta had refused to eat food.

The commanding officer called me and briefed me to persuade him to take his food. If he did not agree, a simple procedure would be implemented. I should get his meal for him on a plate and have it placed before him in front of a witness. I should then order him to consume the meal. If he does not take the meal, that would amount to disobeying a lawful command, and he would be tried as a disciplinary case, as no indiscipline could be allowed from anybody.

I visited the quarter guard and tried to persuade him to take his meals, but he did not agree. I did not like what was happening and wanted to help him; and at the same time, discipline could not be compromised under any circumstances.

"Tell me what your real problem is! I want to help you. Your refusal of food suggests a bigger problem. Let me assure you that by not taking food, you will not solve any problem. You would only make the problem bigger. You must take your food," I told him.

"I cannot take food," He said.

"Why? Are you sick that you cannot take food? You must take food, otherwise there will be a serious problem for you," I told him.

"What problem?" he asked.

"Well, wilful refusal of food is a case of indiscipline; and when a senior officer orders you to take food and you then do not do it, that is disobeying a lawful command, for which you may have to face the court martial," I explained to him.

"Then what?" he asked.

"Then what!? You ask me 'then what'? Don't behave like a kid. You are a brave soldier. Instead of being decorated, you could be dismissed from service, which is highly disgraceful. If you do not know it, I must explain to you that getting court-martialled is very humiliating. For your case there is a possibility of summary court-martial for which one of the punishments is dismissal from service with or without a term of jail.

"For the execution of the judgement, the whole of the unit would be lined up in the parade ground. In front of all the officers and other ranks, the details of the crime and punishment would be read out loudly. Your shoulder straps and regimental badges would be taken away. You would have to change over to civvies immediately; and you would be discharged from your unit and dispatched to your destination at the same time. It is very shameful and demeaning in front of all your colleagues. It is very disgraceful for any soldier.

"Look, Sameer, we have fought a war together and have many a time witnessed death from very close. You have been a very brave soldier, and I respect you for that; that is why I want to help you. Have faith in me; tell me everything truthfully, so that - if possible - you can be helped." I tried to make him understand his situation for the last time.

In the meantime, as I was talking to him, a sentry came to me and informed that some people are standing at the main gate and want to meet Sainik Sameer Das Gupta. I told the sentry to make them sit in the waiting room. When I entered the waiting room, I introduced myself and enquired about them.

One of them was a lady in her mid-forties. She said, "my name is Mrs Shushmeeta Choudhary. Meet my husband and his younger brother; and this is my daughter Roshani. She is engaged to Captain Sameer Das Gupta. We had come to this town for some work and thought that we can meet him. Where is he? Can you call him, please?"

"Where have you come from, madam?" I asked.

"We are coming straight from Kolkata. We have arrived here only this morning. How is Sameer? Can you please call him?" She said again.

"He is not available at the moment. He can meet you in the evening only. Where are you staying?" I asked.

"We are staying at then Hotel Banjara, rooms 13 and 14. At what time he will come? Or we can come here again? You see, we are a bit worried about him. He has not written to us for the past two months. We have written – rather, Roshani has written - many letters to him. He does not reply. I hope he is alright," she sounded worried.

"He is perfectly alright and will certainly meet you in your hotel in the evening," I assured them. Then they left.

I felt that some mystery was unfolding. I went straight to the quarter guard and told him, "Sainik Sameer Das Gupta, your fiancée Roshani, together with her mother, father and uncle, have come to meet you. Now what do you have to say?"

"Sorry, sir, please save me; I am in a big trouble. They are big people, very rich. I have met Roshani two years ago, and we started loving each other. I told her that I am in the army. She asked whether I was a lieutenant or captain, and unwittingly, by mistake, I told her that I am a captain. I got engaged but could never muster the courage to tell her the truth because of the fear of loosing her."

"A real hero in the war, who never was afraid of death, could not find enough courage?" I asked.

"Yes, sir, sometimes life is more frightening than death. Sir, I am in a thick soup. You said that you would help me. Please help me, sir," he pleaded.

I assured him that I would do my best to help him; and I advised him to take his food. He threw himself on the food; obviously he was very hungry. Later when I met my CO ,I told him everything.

"So, it is the love bug. I thought so; that is why I have instructed you to settle this case. You have much experience in this field, don't you, officer? Go and help your soldier," he ordered me.

I liked the old man. He was too good to be a commanding officer; he was a fatherly figure.

In the evening I took Sameer with me to the hotel. I told him to let me talk to them first and not to speak until I told him to do so. I also informed him that it was the time to tell them the truth, and to face whatever happens. He agreed with me completely. Everyone was very happy to meet Sameer. He touched the feet of the elders.

Roshani's father said, "sir, you are very kind to help us meet Sameer. Why did you take the trouble to come all the way?"

"It was essential. There is no question of trouble. We soldiers live and die for each other," I told him.

"Why do you utter negative words? You have done so well in the last war. The whole nation is proud of you soldiers," Roshani said.

In the meantime, tea and snacks were served.

"Thank you very much for saying that, Roshani. And before you say anything else, please allow me to say a few words," I said.

"What do you mean? We can't speak to Sameer? He is engaged to my daughter. Is it not allowed in the army to speak to your relatives?" Roshani's mother got angry.

"Please, madam, please let me say something. You people have come from Kolkata, sensing that he has not been replying to your letters because of some serious problem. I have come to solve that problem. As far as Sameer is concerned, he is a good soldier. He is a wonderful human being. During the war he showed exemplary courage, and the whole unit is proud of him. We all like him very much. You will be happy to know that he has been awarded the Sena Medal, which is very prestigious gallantry award."

"So, you have come to give us this good news. Thank you very much. You army men are so different," said Roshani's mother.

"Thanks. Roshani, tell me how much do you love Sameer?" I asked.

"I can't imagine life without him. I would do anything for him. I will always love him," said Roshani.

"Do you mean that?" I asked.

"Yes, of course I mean that. Was there any doubt in his mind? And why don't you speak, Sameer?" She was very angry.

"Because he is scared of you; he is very scared of losing you," I told her.

"Scared of losing me? Ridiculous! What is this Sameer? How can you think like this? I can marry him just now, right now, here. My parents are also present. They will support me completely. I repeat: I can marry him right now. Why don't you speak, Sameer?" she asked.

Sameer looked at me.

"That is like a good girl. And you gentlemen and madam?" I asked.

"Yes, we are ready. We stand by what Roshani has said. What is wrong? Why are we being misunderstood?" asked Roshani's father.

"Because, unwittingly, Sameer has told a lie to you all, and he was scared that, when the truth comes out, you may all leave him. Now that you have clarified that you accept him as he is, I ask Sameer to tell you the truth," I said.

Sameer said, "first of all I apologise to all of you, and I beg you: Please forgive me that I have inadvertently conveyed to you the impression that I am a captain. My rank is not 'captain.' I am only a Sepoy. Now you may give me any punishment. I will definitely accept any punishment from my own elders, and especially from Roshani, with an open mind."

"Silly, how does that matter? We know you as a good human being and have accepted you in our family. And especially now that you have accepted your mistake, we have more regard for you," said Roshani's mother.

Roshani started crying, "That means you never understood me. I will never talk to you."

I asked the elders to leave the youngsters alone for sometime. We all came out of the room and went to the coffee shop.

"You army people are such a different lot. And to confess to you, we have already decided that after the marriage, he will leave the service and join us in our business," Roshani's father said.

"And for when are you planning for the marriage?" I asked.

"Can we leave that to you, sir? Can you decide on an early date? You have sorted out all the problems so well. Please, make it an auspicious day," Roshani's uncle said.

"There cannot be a more auspicious day than 15 January, which is our Army day. On that day the Chief of Army Staff will present the Sena Medal to Sameer."

"It is done – one hundred per cent fixed. We will also ask Sameer's parents to come here with us to celebrate the marriage - after all, you are from boy's side, sir," Roshani's mother declared.

"But it would be very costly for you, because we are nine hundred Jawans in our unit," I said.

"Never mind, no problem, we will arrange everything. Let it be a grand meal from our side on the Army Day, a splendid grand feast," Roshani's father said. I told them that such a feast is called *Bara Khana* in the army.

14

The Story Tellers

This story began when I was studying in the final year of my B. A. (Honours). Our professor of English literature used to encourage students to speak on certain topics, and he always tried to bring about discussions in the classroom. Once he started a discussion on the subject of 'Love Stories,' and he mentioned that some people think that there is nothing beyond the beauty of their beloveds.

"But, sir, do you think that there is something beyond that also?" The whole class laughed at my question.

"Nonsense, try to be practical. All love vanishes when the question of filling up your belly comes. Before marriage, things are different, but for marriage, you need many things, such as a house, and other necessities of life. The social status of the families is the most important factor. After all you are making new relations and a new standard and set up of your life," he said.

"Sir, those people who are really in love do not trouble themselves with such considerations. No money, no status is bigger than love. The force of love can be felt only when you are in love." I said.

"Whom do you love?" my professor asked.

"That is not relevant. Love is the most personal thing." I replied.

"You seem to be obsessed," remarked my professor.

"Sir, love is an experience which only the most lucky and blessed ones are granted by the Almighty. You call it an obsession, and I call it a gift of life," I said.

"You will fail this year's examinations," he said.

"No Sir, love is not a negative force. You will find me among the top few," I assured him.

Our professor opted out, for a change of subject.

Later, when the class was over, all the students started teasing me about who was the lucky girl, and some of them congratulated me on my good replies to the lecturer. Others pulled my leg that they wanted a few lectures on the subject of love from me.

In the evening, when I met my girlfriend, who was one year junior to me in the college, I told her what had happened in the class.

She said, "Poor professor, but he rightly said one thing - that you seem to be obsessed in love. I do not know what you saw in me. I belong to a very poor family. I do not have any relatives, except my mother, who is a teacher. And you say that you want to marry me?"

"Again you have started the same old story. I told you not to bring up this topic again. And anyway, tell me whether you love me or not?" I asked her.

She said, "I cannot imagine life without you. I was just talking for you. Sometimes I feel that I am the most fortunate girl on this planet to have you. Life is so interesting, so meaningful with you. I can not see anything beyond you."

"That is exactly what I was explaining to our professor." I said.

Four years have passed after this incident. After my graduation, I was commissioned in the army. She had completed her graduation when we both got married. I was posted to the field area where the families were not allowed. Hence my wife had to stay with my parents. I was posted as staff officer at the military headquarters in Ladakh.

The Leh and Ladakh region of Jammu and Kashmir state came into prominence during and after the war with China in 1962. Several miles of snow-covered, mountainous wasteland which is also the world's highest desert, became strategically important territory, to be kept occupied and guarded by the defense forces.

The fastest transport that is available to Leh, for defence personnel, is a seat in the huge transport aircraft of the airforce which flies from Chandigarh. In fact, you cannot call it a seat because you have to sit on sleeping bags and other luggage which are loaded in the middle of the aircraft.

Sitting on personal luggage is not at all comfortable, and at times it is very bumpy. I dozed off soon after the aircraft was airborne. I was woken up, along with other passengers, as we were asked to move back to the tail of the aircraft to facilitate a safe landing. I could not believe my eyes when I looked out of the window and saw the beauty of snow-covered, brilliantly white peaks of the mountains below us. It was enormously exciting to land at the world's highest airport in the middle of the vast cold desert of Leh and Ladakh.

By the time, I reached my room in the officers' mess, I was completely exhausted. The first person whom I encountered there was a wrinkle-faced old Ladakhi who worked in our officers' mess as a waiter. He had brought tea for me. Judging by his frail body, he appeard about seventy years old I wondered why he had not yet retired.

"What is your name?" I asked.

"Rigzin Baba," was his short reply.

"You must been working here for long," I speculated.

"Yes, sir, for the past fifty years," he said.

"Fifty years? And how old are you now?" I asked.

"Sixty years, sir," he replied.

"You mean, you came here when you were ten years old, and you have not retired yet?" I asked.

"Retired? Why retire, sir? Retire for whom? I do not have any family. This mess is my home. You are my family. To serve you is the purpose of my life. You are new here. Please do not throw me out from here. I have lived in this mess for as long as I can remember, and I want to die here." He became agitated.

"Rigzin Baba, do you have hot water here?" I wanted to change the subject. I thought that I had touched a wrong chord.

I met a few officers in the evening. One of the senior officers asked me whether I had met Rigzin Baba.

I said, "yes, why?"

"Oh, he is a very interesting old man. He knows all about Leh and Ladakh. I always ask him where to go and which are the worthwhile places to visit. He is a good guide but he cannot accompany you because of his age. He is a good old man, and talks a lot about the officers who were posted here earlier," he told me.

The next morning Rigzin Baba woke me up with a cup of hot tea. He waited for me to finish it and ask for another cup, as usually everybody did that in this cold place.

"I am sorry, Rigzin Baba, for yesterday's remarks," I apologised.

"What remarks? I have already forgotten them. Please do not say anything about that anymore. You are an officer, and I must obey and serve you. Call me for any service, any time. Tell me, *sahib*, what place do you belong to?" he asked.

"Gujrat, Baba," I told him.

"What place in Gujrat?" he further asked me.

"District Surender Nagar; there is a village which is called Sangali."

"Sangali Patel?" He looked excited.

"Yes, Sangali Patel. How do you know that?" I asked him.

"Tell me, *sahib*, do you know Havildar Raja Ram? Sir, please tell me, do you know Havildar Raja Ram?" he asked.

"Yes, I know him very well. But what about Havildar Raja Ram? Was he ever posted here?" I asked.

"Oh, lord Buddha." And Rigzin Baba caught his head with both his hands and started crying. His thin legs could not hold the weight of his body. He sat down on the ground by his feet. I tried to console him.

"Baba, please tell me: What happened? What has he done to you? Why are you crying? Please get up and sit on the chair. Don't sit on the ground. Please calm down." I helped him to get up and tried to make him sit on the chair.

"Oh *sahib*, I am alright. You are a great man who has brought me the best news of my life." He said.

I was anxious to ask him, "but you must tell me, why did you cry? What did Raja Ram do to you?"

"I will tell you everything. First of all, you tell me. How is he? Rather, how is his wife? Have you ever met her? How is she?" He asked.

I said, "yes, I have met her. She is fine. But why do you ask that? What is she to you?"

"She is my daughter, sir. My only child. Yangchun, my only family member, who left me twenty seven years ago." He again started crying

I gave him water to drink and tried to make him comfortable.

"Sir, tell me about my daughter? How is she?" He asked.

"She is very fine, Baba." I told him.

"Does she ever remember her old father? Twenty seven years ago, Havildar Raja Ram took her away from me. She was very young then - only seventeen years old. He asked me for her hand in marriage. Initially I was hesitant, but when my daughter also insisted I agreed. There were serious objections from the people of our cast, but I did not care. I got them married.

"Raja Ram went on annual leave and took my daughter with him, but he never came back. He deserted his unit. I do not know why he did that. In fact, nobody knows why he deserted his unit. I do not know whether he got scared of our community, or what. He never returned.

"His CO sent the police to his village, but he was not traceable. Initially he did not go to his village for seven years; then I got a letter from my daughter. She wrote that she has been blessed with a baby girl. They had moved to their village – Sangali Patel - and started living with his parents.

"She also wrote to me not to tell his CO so that they may not send the police to their place again. Oh, Lord Buddha, how I crave to see my daughter Yangchun and my grandchild. *Sahibji*, kindly do me a great favour: Please take me there, please, *sahibji*. You have come to me like Lord Buddha Himself. Once, only once, I want to see them. I will pay for my expenses. Please take me to them only once. I want to see my daughter and my little granddaughter Pooja," he pleaded.

I replied, "Yes, Baba, I will definitely take you to them. But would you like to know more about them? Your little granddaughter Pooja is no more a little child now. She has grown up to be a graceful lady."

"Yes, sir, please tell me all that you know about them," he asked to me.

I started narrating. "Baba, after your daughter started living with her in-laws, she served her in-laws well. She also started her studies and completed her B. A. and B. Ed. She got employed as a teacher in a senior secondary school in Surender Nagar city. She is still teaching there, now as a senior teacher.

"Raja Ram started a job in a private company. Their parents had a small house in the village. But Raja Ram and your daughter worked very hard and bought a nice house in Surender Nagar. Both were living happily, and they enrolled their daughter in an English school. About four years ago, Raja Ram fell sick and could not survive.

After completing her school, your granddaughter joined a college in the city. She was very much interested in hockey, and she competed up to the national level. She has grown up to be a very beautiful lady. She has passed her graduation. About six months ago she got married to an Army captain, and she is happily living in her in-laws' house at present."

"Oh, thanks a million, Lord Buddha, for giving me such good news after twenty seven long years, at the tail end of my life. Maybe Lord Buddha kept me alive so that I could see this day. Maybe I have done some good deeds at some time in my life that I have been rewarded with the opportunity to hear about my relatives. Thank you, sir. You have come to me like Lord Buddha himself. Please, *sahib*, would you help me to meet them, please? Kindly do me that great favour, sir." He started crying again.

"Yes, Baba, I will certainly take you to your daughter and your granddaughter. They will also be very happy to meet you. And now that your daughter is living alone, she needs your company. You should go to live with her. Your granddaughter Pooja will also be very happy to meet her grandfather for the first time in her life. But tell me, Baba, would you not like to know whom your granddaughter has married?" I asked.

"He said, "Ah ... oh, Lord Buddha. How great you are to answer all the prayers of my life. How kind and merciful you are. Oh, I understand now. I am sure, sir, my Pooja got married to you. It must be you. Am I right, sir?'

And the two storytellers were locked in an embrace.

"Baba, is it not the time for you to retire from your job?" I asked him, and this time he did not get angry with me.

15

Never Say Die

It was the last wish of my friend Subedar Tehra (thirteen) that I write a book on the unique methods of 'escape' which we had used during the period when both of us were held as prisoners in the 1965 war with Pakistan. I was a young captain at that time and Tehra held the rank of a Naib Subedar.

It is very interesting to know that soldiers in Gurkha regiments are known and called by their army numbers, rather than by their names. The reason is very simple: If you call certain name, like "Bir bahadur" or "Dhan bahadur," for example, there may be twenty people who will answer, "yes, sir." Most of the Nepali ex-servicemen carry their "number names" even to their village and continue to be known by them for the rest of their lives. Although they are called by last four digits of their personal numbers, often only two digits suffice. Sometimes we experience amusing situations in connection with the common names of Gurkhas.

Once Colonel Chouhan was our Regimental Centre Commandant. During his routine visit to the company lines, he asked one of the soldiers whether he knew his name.

The soldier replied promptly, "sorry, sir, I do not know your name, but I know your army number."

The Commandant was much impressed and asked about his number.

"*Chouvan* (fifty four)," was the prompt reply. Such regimental jokes are popular in Gurkha units.

I cannot forget one such number - "Tehra". He was a small, tough and sturdy man with twinkling small eyes. A gentle, honest, loyal, sincere and strong Gurkha - he deserved all the adjectives available in my vocabulary.

Tehra and I were most unfortunate to be taken as prisoners of war by the Pakistan army. But one fortunate aspect for us was that we were both kept together in the prison camp, this circumstance ultimately helped us to escape.

Now it was our Regimental Reunion that gave us another opportunity to meet again after thirty three years. It is a regular custom to hold reunion functions of all the Corps and Regiments of the Indian army in their respective regimental training centres, once every five years. This occasion is a great opportunity for retired colleagues to meet each other and also to interact with their serving younger brethren and share their experiences with them.

At the first glance, I did not quite recognise him because, due to a prolonged illness, he had become very weak. His face was full of wrinkles, and his eyes had further narrowed down. We held each other in a long hug. I felt that his frail body still sported a strong soul.

"How are you, Tehra?" I asked.

"Fighting fit, and how is your spirit, *hazoor* (sir)?" he asked.

By 'spirit,' he meant my wife. My wife was with me at that time, and she too greeted him with warm affection. When we were prisoners, we used to refer to each other's wives as our 'spirits.' The word 'spirit' alluded to the enchanting power of women, as well as to the soul. The soul is taken as immortal and can neither be burnt by fire, nor drowned by water, nor destroyed by any other type of universal force. So, calling our ladies 'spirits' gave us strength during those difficult days.

As far as our survival was concerned, our days of captivity were testing days for us. Whenever we were together, after rigorous physical and mental torture, we used to talk about our wives. That gave us the strength which we needed to withstand the efforts by the enemy to break us. That also gave us the power not to say 'die.'

We used to talk about our love for our wives and about how we had fallen in love with them. I was married before the war, but Tehra was unmarried, and he told me that he would marry none other than his girlfriend 'Dhoop'. It was quite an unusual name, and Tehra said that the name had been given to her by her parents because of her having been very fair at birth. He told me that both of their families had been against the marriage. I suggested to him that after we had managed to escape, and once we are back at our places, they should both make a bid to escape from their families. I promised him all my help to get them married and invited them to come to me whereever I was at that time.

There were many such examples among our ancestors of couples who had run away and had gotten married to live a happy life together. Maharaja Prithvi Raj Chouhan, after he had made a daring escape, picked up his beloved princess on his famous horse Chetak, and then reached his kingdom with her. During her *swaymver* (a marriage where the bride has the right to choose her husband), she had put the *jaimala* (flower garland) around the neck of the statue of Maharaja Prithvi Raj Chouhan. After reaching the capital of his kingdom, he got married to her against the wishes of her father who was a very powerful king. I narrated the sacred example of Lord Krishna. After princess Rukmani had prayed and begged the Lord to save her from being married against her wishes, the lord came personally to help her escape in his chariot, and he got married to her as she had wished.

Such stories strengthened our confidence that we would escape from captivity one day, that the happy days of independence will return, and that we will live together with our people again.

The love story of Dhoop and Tehra was very interesting. They both believed that they had been husband and wife in their previous lives also. And hence, nobody could separate them in this life. He was very confident that we would be successful in escaping and would get married only to her. I did not know much about, and also did not believe in, the theory of last life and rebirth. But Tehra used to tell me about the 'theory of rebirth' with great conviction. Although I did not understand much, I always used to listen to him patiently. Many a time he even talked about the 'theory of parallel life'.

He once said, "sir, at this moment, as we are talking to each other here today, exactly like this, in some other universe, there are two people like you and me taken as prisoners of war and are discussing the same thing in similar words. The best example is sitting before a mirror. Imagine that we are both sitting in front of a large mirror and watching ourselves talking to each other.

Similarly, we are also doing the same thing in another world. We only cannot watch the second form of ourselves. There are enemies; there is a sentry posted to guard us as all this is happening.

The point is that one must believe in the theory. Since you do not have faith, you cannot see or feel anything. I have faith; therefore I can feel the reality. When you achieve 'realisation,' you will cease to feel hurt by the beatings and torture of the enemy. In fact, you may even begin to forgive your enemies, because they are doing their duty in trying to break us – they want to obtain as much information as possible for their country.

Do you remember Bapu Gandhji? He even forgave the man who killed him and said that God may pardon the killer, as he did not know whatever he was doing."

Although I did not believe in everything that he said, I found his theories very interesting, and they gave us tremendous strength to withstand the torture.

Now as we meet and I was reflecting on his points, I had forgotten to ask him about his wife. After some time I asked him, "Where is your Dhoop, Tehra?"

"Right here, standing outside your room, hazoor," he replied.

"What the bloody hell? You made her wait outside for such a long time?" I asked.

"What do you mean by 'wait for a long time'? We have hardly met, sir. She herself chose not to disturb us; otherwise she does not need any permission to come to your room. After all, it was with your help that she became my *dulhan* (wife)," he said.

I made a dash outside and asked Tehra's wife to come inside. I had seen her as a young bride, and now I saw a graceful mature lady. We looked after her with great regard and affection. We discussed many old episodes and relived the memories of bygone days. I asked her about their family and other things, and especially about his theory of rebirth, and so on. She, too, believed in that theory, and she told me of a few experiences which had confirmed her belief. She mentioned that during our days of captivity, she had dreamt about how cruelly Tehra was being treated by the enemy and also that he had a close companion with him who would ultimately help him escape. I felt good to meet them after such a long time.

The reunion functions were to last for five days. Tehra told me that they had especially come to this reunion to meet me, so that they could be with us on 'the last day.' I did not understand what he meant by 'the last day' but left that question without asking as there were, in any case, many other mysterious things about them that I did not quite understand.

I lifted his left hand and kissed it with great affection, because that was the hand which had lost all its fingers during the torture by the enemy. All five fingers of his left hand were cut off one by one in my presence. It was done in front of me with a view to frightening me and thus extracting the information.

Later, when they had not succeeded to break him by cutting off the fingers of his left hand one by one, they cut off all the toes of my left foot in a similar manner. But we remained true to our word; the enemy could not extract any information from us.

"Sir, let me feel your left foot," he said.

"It is in the same condition my friend. Once cut off, the fingers never grow back," I told him.

"But, please let me touch your foot," he requested.

When I removed my shoe and the socks, he bent down and touched my left foot with his forehead. I felt that such respect from a soldier who was himself one of the best example of bravery was more valuable than any gallantry award.

We held each other in an embrace for a long time. It was like spiritual healing touch to our sick bodies. I felt that Tehra was working his magic to overcome all my physical weaknesses and to strengthen my body. It was an amazing experience which I cannot describe in words.

In fact, I owed to him all my powers of withstanding the enemy torture during our days of captivity. He was the real source of strength for me. He also expressed similar sentiments about my being with him during that painful period of our life. Any soldier would prefer to be killed in the war rather than become a prisoner of war, but there are certain circumstances in which you cannot avoid what destiny holds for you.

As I met him now, after such a long time, I was feeling greatly contented and at peace. I could not utter a word of gratitude to him. Professional soldiers never say 'thank you' to each other on such occasions.

It was a great experience for me to realise the power of silence. We just looked at each other for a long while, and we chose not to say anything during those moments. My thoughts drifted back to the old memories. I started thinking again about the days of my captivity.

I had argued with the enemies for better treatment according to the Geneva Convention, but they rudely said that they did not care about any convention. They meted out to us the worst type of punishment and called us the dirtiest of names.

We had both made a pledge, holding each others' hands, that we would not give them any information even if they should break our bodies to the pieces. No force would ever break our spirits.

It was the first day of our captivity when Tehra asked me what our duty was after being taken as prisoners of war. I told him that our duty was to try to escape from the captivity and not to disclose any information to them under any circumstances. Under the Geneva Convention, the only information that we were supposed to give them was our army number, rank, and name.

We had put all our thoughts together to plan the escape. Tehra suggested that we should dig a tunnel. I knew that the task was not impossible, because we were kept close to the border in 'Pakistan Occupied Kashmir.'

To acquire the digging tools was also not very difficult because we were used by the enemy for digging trenches everyday.

Tehra told me of a similar episode in his father's life during the period of the Second World War. His father was a NCO (non-commissioned officer) in the 'Royal Indian Army Ordnance Corps' and was posted in an Indian

Garrison Depot in the village called Kangla-Tongbi, in South-East Burma. The Japanese army had launched a massive attack, with large number of soldiers, on a small force that was holding defence stores. A few brave ordnance personnel who were holding the defence stores fought back and repelled the attack, causing heavy casualties on the enemy.

The Japanese returned on the third night with a bigger force for a counter attack. Unfortunately, the Japanese took his father and six other soldiers as prisoners of war. Soon after being taken as prisoners of war, they started planning their escape.

The whole area was full of thick jungle. They were inspired by the big rats in that area. Those rats worked day and night, digging tunnels to carry food which they stole from the army cookhouses. A team of seven spent five nights digging a fifty yards long tunnel. Once they had gotten out of sight of the enemy, my father and the other six persons passed the following six nights walking, and they spent their daytime hiding in the treetops. They had to cross the main river of Burma, which is known as 'Chinwin,' and its tributary, which is known as 'Seating.' That escape looked like an impossible task but Tehra's father and the others accomplished it and returned home safely.

We were greatly inspired by this fantastic example, and we decided to dig the tunnel. The tunnel had to be just long enough for crossing the fencing or wall where one is jailed; once one has crossed that barrier, one can use other means to get away.

We started digging at about twelve o'clock in one dark night. The digging turned out to be extremely difficult because the area was very rocky, and motor-operated tools would have been needed to break the stones. Anyway, we did not want to abandon our plan without having tried our best. Unluckily, on the third night, we were caught digging.

That discovery of our escape attempt by the enemy was followed by very severe punishment. But our determination was stronger than the might of the enemy.

We were reminded of a song which was commonly sung by our respected forefathers during the freedom struggle.

"*Sarfroshi ki tamanna, ab hamare dil men hai,*
Dekhana hai zore kitna bazu-e-katil men hai."

(We have now made a vow to sacrifice our heads, and we will dare to see how strong the arms of the enemy are.)

When we were youngsters, we had seen our elders being taken to hospitals after they had been injured in the beatings by the English rulers. They used to re-join the agitation after having only slightly recovered from the injuries which they had sustained.

I told Tehra about the greatest example of extreme sacrifice by the tenth Guru, Shri Gobind Singh, Maharaj, who had sacrificed his father, mother and all his four young sons for the sake of the nation.

During that difficult period and in that terrible situation, in which we both were, it was only wise to remember the great examples of those sacrifices and to be proud of the rich heritage that we Indians have. Our motivation was at its highest, and nothing could stop us from achieving our objective.

After having failed once, we thought of other ways to escape. We decided to make an attempt at outwitting the enemy by making a dash to the border whenever our guards took us outside the fencing for physical labour. But unfortunately that also did not work out.

I told my companion that I am going to try another approach, but that, before I do so, we have to discover the personal weaknesses of each individual sentry, and of anybody else with whom we came into contact in that prison.

The in-charge of that jail was a Subedar. During his routine visit to the prison camp, I asked him; "*Sahib*, from your stature and smart appearance and your name it seems that you are from the generation of brave Khans."

"Yes, my father was very brave and famous," He boasted.

"To which place do you belong, *sahib*?" I tried to prolong the conversation.

"Oh, I belong to the famous NWFP (North-Western Frontier Province). You can say, the Peshawar district area, which else?" He sounded very proud of his place.

"That is the sacred land of a great people. In fact, my father was also from that area. He used to tell us stories about the bravery and large-heartedness of the people in that area. I was told that they were very fond of a variety of meat and chicken dishes."

"Yes, yes, of course. Tell me, have these *kameenas* (mean people) ever given you any meat dish so far, or are they keeping you alive on *ghass-phoos* (vegetarian eatables) only?"

"No problem, *sahib*, we can hope to get Peshavari type cooked meat on your birthday," I said.

"No problem, I can celebrate my birthday tomorrow. Don't worry you will get that tomorrow." He assured us.

"*Sahib*, can I ask the name of your respected father?" I asked.

"Oh, why not, everyone knew him in the whole province. Who does not know Khan Bahadur Saleem Beg, *Sahib*?" He started twisting his moustache.

"Ah, I think my father had mentioned about your great father to me. He has thrashed the English rulers during the freedom struggle. I think you are related to Sarhaddi Gandhi (Gandhiji from the frontier area), the most honorable Khan Abdul Gaffar Khan *Sahib*. God bless his noble soul," I said with all my humility.

"Yes, of course they fought for the nation and won their freedom from the *Firungees*" (the English rulers of India before freedom was attained), he said.

"Yes, *sahib*, they fought for our nation, and today we brothers are fighting each other. There was the big conspiracy of the English people to divide and rule. Our forefathers, who were born and brought up like brothers, and always stood together and shared the happiness and the sorrows of each other, have now started killing each other. *Sahib*, don't you see in me a lost son of a close friend of your respected father?" I asked.

I saw drops of tears in his eyes. He left after some time. I told Tehra that I have touched the right chord, and that the plan was working. From that day onwards, we started getting better food and better treatment. Even the number of guards was reduced. The jailer visited us more often. I took pains to humour his ego, and I never lost an opportunity to touch him emotionally. We began to realise that we had won his confidence, and were given a little more freedom. I told Tehra that we are perhaps about to achieve our objective, and that we must be prepared to make a dash to the border anytime, when we get an opportunity. It would have to be our best effort, because it was a matter of life and death.

Our opportunity came on the real birthday of the jail's in-charge. I requested one of our regular sentries to get a few flowers from the bush outside our jail for making a present to the *sahib*.

The sentry demanded money for the favour. That gave me the idea that he could␣the bribed. I told him that I would give him our two wristwatches and a gold ring which we had at that moment and arrange a payment of ten thousand rupees to him if he would let us cross the border. Ten thousand rupees was a big amount in 1965.

Initially he hesitated but I told him a foolproof plan which would not implicate him in our escape. I told him that one of the nights when he is on other duties, we would cut the fencing and run away. But before going, we would make our sleeping place look as if we both are sleeping under the blankets. After some time, he should request one of his companions to take his place for a few minutes, and – upon returning – he should call out that he saw us running and start firing in the direction where we would possibly have gone.

He was apprehensive about the payment, but I told him that in any case, if we remain captive, he will not get anything. But officers of the Indian army are always true to their word, and if he believes my word, he will get his money. I told him that the payment can be made through one of his relatives in India, or by any other means of his choice. He gave me the name and address of a relative of his in India.

Thus we bought our freedom and returned to our country. For some time we were both assigned the duty of giving detailed talks about the whole episode in various army units and training centres. We had a small message for everyone.

'Never say die, for as long as you live.'

We served our normal tenure of service, and now after our retirement, it was the first time that we had a reunion. I felt grateful to the government for holding regular reunion functions and arranging opportunities for old companions to meet.

A night before the last day of the reunion celebrations, we had a grand dinner - called 'Bara khana' - for all the ranks

Tehra was in a special mood on that day, and we talked a lot about our days as prisoners of war.

Tehra said; "Why don't you write a book on 'How to escape'? I don't think that the methods which you have applied have been written about in any book. You have a flair for writing, too. Do it for the sake of others."

"That is not a bad idea, and I think, I will do it some day," I said.

He got annoyed and shouted at me, "Some day? Do you think that time will wait for you? Look at our ages. I think that we have lived enough and should make place for others. Otherwise this earth will get unbalanced. We have played our part and should make a respectable exit now. I have the wish to depart from this life on your shoulders. You see, many a time we have seen death from very close. In fact, I must confess to you today that during those days in prison I had a secret wish that, if the enemy decided to kill us, I would die first and then be cremated by you. These are the relations of many lives, that is why we met again in this life."

He again started talking to me about his theories of 'rebirth' and 'parallel life,' and he carried on till very late in the night. I suggested to him to get some sleep because we had to attend the *Yaadgaar Parade* (a parade ceremony by the armed forces in the memory of dead soldiers) early in the morning.

On the next morning when I got up and was trying to get dressed, I was told that the *Yaadgaar Parade* has been postponed to 5:00 p.m. on the next day. When I asked for the reason I was told that retired Subedar major and honorary Lieutenant Tehra and his wife had died last night. I rushed to the hospital and was told that they had suffered a massive heart attack during their sleep and that their bodies had been sent for postmortem.

I recollected his remarks about being with me on the 'last day' and also his wish to complete his last journey on my shoulders.

My frail, old and sick body did not feel much difficulty in giving a shoulder for carrying the remains of the brave soldier, and my close friend, Tehra. Other young officers tried to take the turn from me, but I insisted on taking him to his destination. I felt that his spirit was persuading me to play my part to the finish, to help him in making the final escape.

He was cremated with full army honours and the Yaadgaar Parade of that year was held in the honour of the brave Tehra and other soldiers who had left for their heavenly abode.

I could not come to a clear conclusion, whether meeting him in this life was a mere coincidence or whether there was any connection to his theories of rebirth and parallel life. Whatever may be the truth, the moments spent with him have become immortal in my most cherished memories.